An Executive's Guide to Disciplined Agile

Winning the Race to Business Agility

Scott W. Ambler and Mark Lines

DEDICATION

For Louise, Brian and Katherine, thank you for your love and support.

- Mark

For Beverley and Olivia, the best family I could have hoped for.

- Scott

ISBN: 1539852962
ISBN-13: 978-1539852964

CONTENTS

Acknowledgements

We'd like to thank the following people for their feedback and insights that went into making this book the best that we could make it: Khurshid Akbar, Beverley Ambler, Jeff Anderson, Alex Ballarin, Klaus Boedker, Bjorn Gustafsson, Rod Bray, Daniel Gagnon, Matt Everard, Louise Lines, Glen Little, Jason Little, Alex Papworth, Valentin-Tudor Mocanu, David Shapiro, Paul Sims, and Jon Smart.

Cover design by Beverley Ambler

PREFACE

We've written yet another book about agile (YABAA). Great, just what the world needs. ;-)

Seriously though, this book is different because most of us are not in a position to custom evolve an agile culture in a start-up company. This agile book is for the rest of us, people working in existing organizations that have a long and deep history. In other words, less than ideal situations. These include financial institutions, retailers, government agencies, telecoms, restaurant chains, transport companies, and many other organizations that have to contend with legacy cultures, legacy organization structures, and legacy information technology (IT) applications and infrastructures.

Why You Need to Read This Book

There are three fundamental forces in the marketplace today:

1. **Every business is a software business**. We used to say that software is eating the world, but the fact is that for most companies software is the world. Tesla's competitive value isn't electric cars, instead it's Tesla's ability to upgrade and enhance those cars through software. Starbucks now competes on software – people pay and now even order via their phones, and they're being motivated to buy more to earn loyalty stars. Gone are the days where IT could be treated like a utility, one that more often than not was outsourced in the belief that you needed to focus on your core competencies and IT didn't make it onto that list. These days being competent at IT is mere table stakes at best, you need to excel at IT if you hope to become an industry leader.

2. **Every industry is being disrupted.** When we start working with a new customer one of the first questions we ask is "What keeps you up at night?" Interestingly, it's been over two years since anyone told us they were afraid of their traditional competitors. Everyone tells us they're afraid of disruptors, new competitors entering their market space using technologies in new ways. Financial firms fear disruption by new Fintech competitors. Retailers are being disrupted by online shopping with malls at risk of being shuttered. Healthcare is being disrupted by artificial intelligence (AI) and 3D printing. It is clear that your organization needs to make a hard decision very soon – Do you want to be the disruptor or the disrupted?

3. **Agile firms dominate**. Becoming an agile business – an adaptive, responsive, and learning organization – is your true goal. Business agility requires true agility across all of your organization, not just software development, not just DevOps, and not just IT. There isn't a single industry now that either isn't dominated by agile businesses or isn't under threat of disruption by new agile competitors. Not one.

As a result of these three forces this book has a heavy focus on IT, but recognizes that IT by itself is insufficient. This book walks you through the four levels of the Disciplined Agile (DA) 3 framework that lead to enterprise agility:

1. **Disciplined Agile Delivery (DAD)**. DAD describes a context-sensitive, lightweight and robust approach to solution delivery from beginning to end – DAD takes the mystery out of how agile software development works in practice in enterprise-class settings.

2. **Disciplined DevOps**. This is the streamlining of IT solution development and IT operations activities, and supporting enterprise-IT activities, to provide more effective outcomes to an organization.

3. **Disciplined Agile IT (DAIT)**. This is a collaborative, learning-oriented, and adaptive approach to the delivery of IT services and products that focuses on supporting your overall organization in value creation and delivery.

4. **Disciplined Agile Enterprise**. Such an organization is able to sense and respond swiftly to changes in the marketplace. It does this through an organizational culture and structure that facilitates change within the context of the situation that it faces. Such organizations require a learning mindset in the mainstream business and underlying lean and agile processes to drive innovation.

More importantly, we show how all of this fits together in an adaptive, streamlined whole – the days of locally optimizing individual processes through disparate and contradictory "books of knowledge (BoKs)" are over. Yes, we want to leverage and evolve these BoKs but no, we can no longer afford to be driven by them. To succeed in today's hyper-competitive environments we must optimize the whole organization.

Who This Book is For

We've written this book for three groups of people:

1. **Business leaders**. This book provides a vision for the organizations behaviors required to succeed in today's marketplace. Although a significant focus is on IT, we must also streamline business operations, governance, procurement, human resources (HR), and other aspects of your organization to be competitive.

2. **IT leaders**. This book answers fundamental questions such as: How can we streamline all of IT? How does it all fit together? How can agile and lean strategies be applied to all aspects of IT, not just software development? How do we deal with other complexities such as compliance, vendor management, budgeting, and offshoring? How can we improve each aspect of IT in parallel yet still collaborate effectively?

3. **Big-picture agilists**. This is anyone with the desire to understand how agile truly works in enterprise-class settings, who recognize that we need to look beyond agile software development if we're going to succeed in today's marketplace.

This book is for people with the courage to look at the bigger picture, because frankly the big picture tends to be very ugly in practice. It's for people willing to consider all aspects of their organization and who realize that IT is a key enabler of business agility. It's for people who realize that context counts, that everyone faces a unique situation and will be agile in their own unique way, that one process does not fit all. It's for people who realize that, although they are in a unique situation, others have faced similar situations before and have identified a variety of strategies that you can adopt and tailor – you can reuse the process learnings of others and thereby invest your energies into adding critical business value to your organization.

1 INTRODUCTION

Many processes, or methods if you prefer that term, prove to be a prescriptive, one size fits all cookbook. There is often significant marketing rhetoric around the flexibility of the process and how you can tailor it to do anything you want, but in the end they always seem to tell you the "one best way" of doing things and offer very little advice around what your other options are. It is little wonder why so many people are bitter about process these days, yet the hard reality is that we all follow some form of process to do our work. Shouldn't we try to find a way to tailor and evolve our processes to be as streamlined and effective as possible? That's what this book is all about.

In many ways Disciplined Agile (DA) is very different from other process offerings. DA is a process decision framework, not a process or methodology. Adoption of DA has really taken off in the last few years, largely because it provides an evolutionary approach towards continuous delivery and DevOps while providing guidance such as agile governance to lend rigor and structure to the overall approach. The approach enables organizations to develop and evolve competitive value streams to provide products and services to their customers. Jon Smart, the Agility Lead of Barclays Group, says it well "We adopted Disciplined Agile across Barclays worldwide because it provides the consistency and structure of a framework with the flexibility of approach at the team level". In other words, you have the same discipline to live within reasonable governance and constraints that you would expect in a banking situation, but you are free to figure out the details yourselves. Barclays executed the fastest agile transformation of its size seen to date, with currently over 1,000 teams using DA globally.

This chapter is organized into the following topics:
- It's only getting harder
- The racing car metaphor
- The Disciplined Agile framework
- From scaling to enterprise agile
- Value streams
- Complex adaptive systems
- The (false) promise of bodies of knowledge (BoKs)
- Your improvement journey
- The final destination: Business agility

It's Only Getting Harder

The need to improve the way that your organization operates, including improving the way that you're organized and the way that you work, is imperative. It seems that every day there are changes in the business environment, such as new technologies that offer new opportunities or new competitors with business strategies that threaten to disrupt your existing value streams. These external challenges include:

- Customers expect to be delighted, not just satisfied
- Digital transformation, the use of technology to radically improve the way that you serve your customers, is sweeping all industries
- The pace of technical change is staggering
- The pace of business change is increasing – Value streams emerge, evolve, and disappear much more rapidly than just a few short years ago
- Overall complexity is increasing as the result of rapid change
- Security threats are increasing and attacks are becoming more sophisticated
- Established agile organizations are expanding into new industries and becoming disruptive competitors
- Disruptive competitors are blindsiding established organizations and often cutting into the most profitable aspects of their business
- Dramatic political changes are afoot around the world

For example, within the finance industry in particular we have witnessed first-hand a real urgency, indeed panic, by companies to aggressively adopt agile and lean across their organizations. Speaking with their leadership, they universally cite the FinTech revolution as the source of their concern. Recently a new class of company that does not have the cost burden of traditional brick and mortar companies has begun to deliver financial products over the web, collectively known as FinTech companies. They are also applying new technologies such as blockchain to further disrupt the financial industry. In our first book we made the somewhat controversial statement that "those who fail to adopt Agile risk going out of business". Five years later, we not only continue to believe this is so, but we would go further and suggest that those who fail to evolve their solution delivery capabilities to support the continuous delivery of value to stakeholders risk going out of business.

Of course it doesn't stop there. Your organization may also be afflicted by many internal challenges, including:

- Organizational structures that reflect long, drawn-out processes
- An aging workforce, a particular problem within IT because much of the knowledge of your core solutions resides in the head of people about to retire
- Organizational silos, each of which have their own priorities and ways of working
- Misalignment between business and IT results in waste and lost opportunities
- Misalignment within IT is common, with various technical silos each having their own "body of knowledge" – more on this later
- Technical debt, quality problems in your systems and overall infrastructure, make it difficult to evolve them quickly to support shifting value streams
- Staff attraction and retention is becoming increasingly harder
- Traditional organizational cultures struggle to address the needs of the new and changing environment you face
- Governance processes based on documentation-heavy, waterfall processes are choking the life out of teams
- Overly specialized staff struggle to evolve with the times
- Workspaces lack flexibility and often inhibit collaboration

One organization that is in the process of adopting a Disciplined Agile approach is the Insurance Corporation of British Columbia (ICBC). Like every other organization that has been in business for many years they suffer from the usual challenges surrounding technical debt and traditional culture. Recognizing the need to optimize the whole organization, not just agile teams, they have restructured their IT division to create long-term stable, cross functional teams aligned to lines of business. They have also redesigned workspaces and where possible collocated their teams. In addition they have been actively investing in training and coaching to help evolve their culture and improve the ways that they work, and they have started into paying down their technical debt in a responsible manner. What makes them stand out, particularly for a North American company, is that they are unionized. Often, the existence of a union increases the friction between workers and management and for the most part decreases the organization's overall ability to respond in the marketplace. In this case the coaches are working with the union to gain their support to help their members gain agile skills and to fairly rework job descriptions to reflect Disciplined Agile roles.

The Racing Car Metaphor

Since 2001 agilists have been focused on finding ways to improve how software is developed. We've adopted fundamental strategies such as regular coordination meetings, regular demos, product owners, developer regression testing, retrospectives, and incremental releases of working software. Disciplined teams have adopted more advanced strategies such as active stakeholder participation, continuous integration (CI), test-driven development, continuous documentation, continuous deployment, measured improvement, and incremental releases of consumable solutions (to name a few). We experiment with new techniques to learn what works for us in the situation that we face, improving our approach as we do so in an incremental kaizen-style manner over time. In effect we are finding ways to tune our "development engines" so that we can deliver more valuable functionality, to reduce our cycle time, and to be more productive as a team. This is very similar to a Formula One team who over the years improves their racing car engine to deliver more power and more speed for less fuel consumption so as to help them win the race.

But agile software development alone isn't sufficient. We see too many agile teams, who on their own are doing a great job at improving the way that they work, get bogged down by their organizational environment. This is particularly true in established enterprises that have been in operation for decades and sometimes even centuries. The software developers are agile, but you still have a "quality assurance (QA)" group that insists on manual testing based on a detailed requirements document. Or it takes days and sometimes weeks to release a new version of a system into production because of your existing release management practices. You've got this great agile team, a great car engine, but you've put it into an organizational tractor. Is it any wonder you're not seeing the desired improvements? Many organizations have come to realize that agile software development alone isn't enough and now are focusing on DevOps. They've increased the scope of their improvement efforts because they realize that their race car engines really need to be put into a race car.

But this isn't sufficient either. Just like a race car needs a driver and pit crew to operate it, your DevOps strategy is part of your overall IT strategy. If your IT governance approach is based on traditional thinking that requires teams to jump through documentation-oriented "quality gates" then that's the equivalent of a pit crew putting square wheels onto the car and then holding the driver accountable for losing the race. Similarly your DevOps efforts won't scale without a flexible, supporting enterprise architecture strategy. Just like your race car requires an effective team to run it in a race, your DevOps strategy requires a supporting IT team and infrastructure for it to be effective.

But this still isn't enough. A race car and team is of little value if there's nowhere to race! They are part of a larger racing business which has multiple value streams through which they generate revenue: They make money from ticket sales, from advertisers, from merchandising, and from many other sources. Similarly, your IT department is part of your larger organization, involved with and supporting many value streams from which you make money.

So, to summarize, an engine is part of a race car that is evolved and operated by a team of people and this race car team is part of the overall racing business. Similarly, our software/solution delivery teams are part of an overall DevOps effort, which in turn is part of your IT strategy. Your IT strategy is one aspect of your overall organizational strategy. All of this must work together smoothly, given the challenges described earlier, in order for you to have a truly agile organization. And, on top of that, you need to accomplish this given the myriad of internal and external challenges that you face. How hard could that be?

The Disciplined Agile Framework

Enter the Disciplined Agile (DA) process decision framework. DA provides light-weight guidance to help organizations streamline their information technology (IT) and business processes in a context-sensitive manner. It does this by showing how the various activities such as solution delivery, operations, enterprise architecture, portfolio management, finance, security, legal, and many others work together. The framework also describes what these activities should address, provides a range of options for doing so, and describes the tradeoffs associated with each option. In effect, DA provides the process foundation for business agility. As you can see in Figure 1.1, there are four levels to the DA framework:

Figure 1.1. The scope of the DA framework.

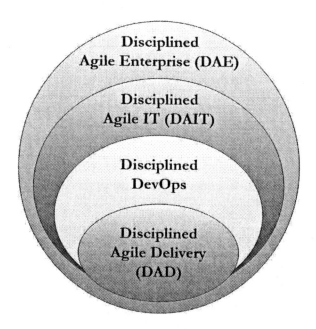

1. **Disciplined Agile Delivery (DAD).** DAD addresses all aspects of solution delivery, from beginning to end, in a streamlined manner. This includes initial modelling and planning, forming the team, securing funding, continuous architecture, continuous testing, continuous development, and governance all the way through the lifecycle. The framework includes support for multiple delivery lifecycles, including but not limited to a basic/agile lifecycle based on Scrum, a lean lifecycle based on Kanban, two modern agile lifecycles for continuous delivery, and an exploratory lifecycle based on Lean Startup [Ries]. This is the topic of Chapter 3.
2. **Disciplined DevOps.** This is the streamlining of IT solution development and IT operations activities, and supporting enterprise-IT activities, to provide more effective outcomes to an organization. Disciplined DevOps is overviewed in Chapter 4 and an overview of the workflow is shown in Figure 1.2.
3. **Disciplined Agile IT (DAIT).** DAIT addresses how to apply agile and lean strategies to all aspects of IT. This

includes IT-level activities such as IT operations, support, data management, reuse engineering, and other capabilities. This is the topic of Chapter 5 and an overview of the workflow is shown in Figure 1.3.

4. **Disciplined   Agile Enterprise**.   A   Disciplined Agile Enterprise is able to anticipate and respond swiftly to changes in the marketplace. It does this through an organizational culture and structure that facilitates change within the context of the situation that it faces. Such organizations require a learning mindset in the mainstream business and underlying lean and agile processes to drive innovation. This is the topic of Chapter 6 and the workflow for which is overviewed in Figure 1.4.

Figure 1.2 The workflow of Disciplined DevOps.

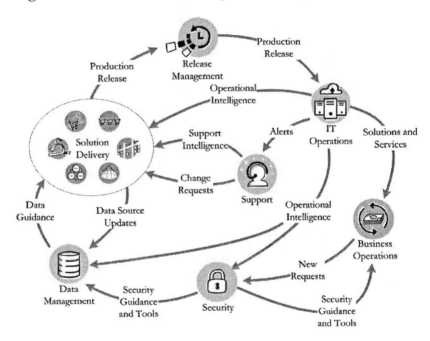

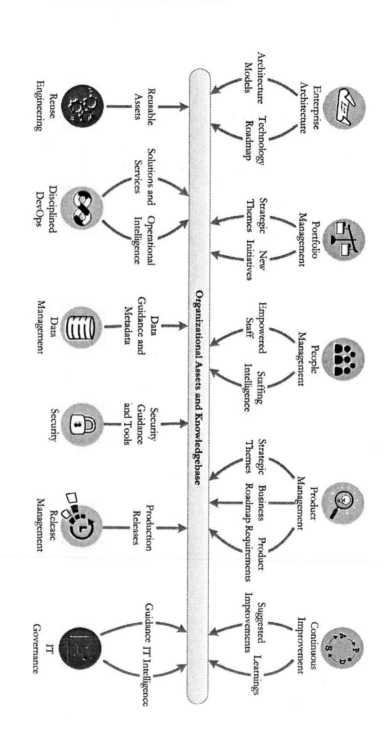

Figure 1.3 The high-level workflow of Disciplined Agile IT (DAIT).

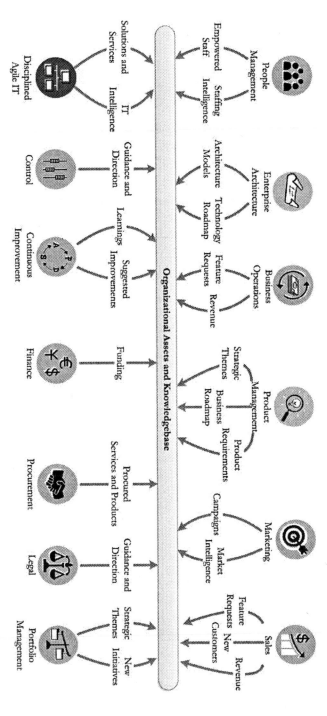

Figure 1.4. The high-level workflow of a Disciplined Agile Enterprise.

From Scaling to Enterprise Agile

What does it mean to scale agile? The answer to this question depends on who you ask. For example, some people will tell you that scaling agile means applying agile strategies to a large software development team or to a geographically distributed software development team. To others scaling agile means applying agile strategies across a lot of software development teams and to others scaling agile means you apply agile strategies to your organization as a whole. As a result the DA framework distinguishes between two types of "agility at scale":

1. **Tactical agility at scale (to deal with context)**. This is the application of agile and lean strategies on individual Disciplined Agile Delivery (DAD) teams. This includes the ability to apply agile on teams of all sizes, on teams that are geographically distributed, on teams facing regulatory compliance, on teams addressing a complex domain (problem space), on teams applying complex technologies, on teams where outsourcing may be involved, and combinations thereof. An important implication of this is that because you are likely to have delivery teams facing different situations, these teams will be following different tailorings of DAD – context counts.

2. **Strategic agility at scale (to deal with organizational breadth)**. This is the broad application of agile and lean strategies across your entire organization. From an IT point of view this includes Disciplined DevOps and Disciplined Agile IT (DAIT) in general. From an enterprise point of view this includes all divisions and teams within your organization, not just your IT department, what we call the Disciplined Agile Enterprise.

You Offer Value Streams to Your Customers

We've used the term "value stream" in several places already, so time to define it. A value stream is the sequence of activities an organization undertakes to deliver a product or service to a customer (or a family of related products and services). Most value streams are highly cross functional: the transformation of a customer request or internal idea to a product or service flows through many functional departments or work teams within the organization [MartinOsterling]. As an example, getting a car repaired might include making an appointment, checking in to drop off the car, ordering parts, repairs, pickup, and payment. The value stream touches many cross-functional business processes and possibly multiple IT solutions, in this case to handle appointment scheduling, labor management, customer management, parts inventory, and billing. A value stream may be internal to a company, or it may include external suppliers in addition to the internal processes required to leverage them. A value stream starts and ends with the customer in mind. What problems or needs do they have? What can we do to fulfill them? How can we delight the customer in how we do so? How can we do better? All critical questions you should continuously ask as an organization.

There's three important points we'd like to make about value streams right now. First, a Disciplined Agile Enterprise is built around value streams, not project streams. Two of the five Disciplined Agile Delivery lifecycles are structured to deliver projects in an agile manner but the framework quite clearly recommends moving away from projects[1] to continuous delivery aligned to value streams. Yes, you may still have projects (although many organizations are now moving away from the concepts of projects, particularly in the IT space) but your primary focus will be on the ongoing efforts around value streams. Second, value streams encompass all the people, resources, and activities required. From the point of view of DA, that implies that a value stream will encompass activities such as solution delivery, operations and support of that solution, product management for the products that support the value stream, governance within the value stream, security, and so on. Yet at the same time there are organizational aspects of these activities that go beyond value streams. Third, value streams have varying lifespans – some only a few months, some a few years, and some decades or more – that go beyond the normal scope of a project and beyond any annual budgeting processes you may currently have. To properly support value streams you will likely need to improve your organizational processes and structures.

Your Organization is a Complex Adaptive System

A Disciplined Agile Enterprise (DAE) is a complex adaptive system. A complex adaptive system is a system in which a perfect understanding of the individual parts does not automatically convey a perfect understanding of the whole system's behavior [CAS]. DAEs are complex because they are a dynamic network of interacting teams, see Figure 1.5, where the overall behavior of the organization is not predicted by the behavior of the individual teams. Having said that, the individual teams are still working towards fulfilling the common goal of the DAE – to delight their customers. When this behavior is positive it's often referred to as synergy, when this behavior is negative it's referred to as a failing

---

[1] This is referred to as the #NoProjects movement.

organization. DAEs are adaptive because individuals and teams self-organize and learn from their experiences, and hopefully from the experiences of others.

Figure 1.5. Every team collaborates with and affects other teams.

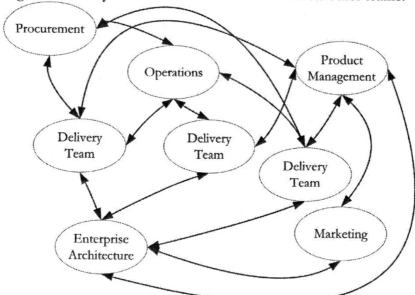

This is important because Disciplined Agile thrives when your organization embraces the fact that it is a CAS. Disciplined Agile is about self-organization, improvement, and collaboration amongst other things. Our self-organizing teams will each need to own their process, agile slang for being given process autonomy, and will evolve that process as the team learns from their experiences. Changes in the way that a team works will potentially impact the other teams that it interacts with, those teams will then learn and evolve, which will potentially impact other

Uniqueness over Commonality
Your organization is made up of a collection of interacting teams, each of which follows a process that is unique to them. The team process evolves over time as the team learns, and each team will have their own specific priorities. Yet, even though your teams are unique they won't be radically different from each other. Hopefully teams collaborate with one another, they will work towards your organization's goal(s), and they will be governed fairly.

teams, and so on. The 2016 Agility at Scale study [AoS2016] found that 96% of agile teams reported that they needed to collaborate with one or more groups outside of their team in order to do their work successfully, so this is quite common in practice.

Beware The (False) Promise of Bodies of Knowledge (BoKs)

Disciplined Agile Enterprises (DAEs) are complex adaptive systems of interconnected, collaborating teams of people working towards a common goal. An important implication of this interconnectedness is that to be effective you need to improve your overall strategy, not just portions of it. This is very different than the traditional strategy of divide and conquer, the days of allowing teams to locally optimize their processes in isolation through adopting disparate and contradictory "bodies of knowledge (BoKs)" are over. Table 1.1 lists a sampling of the dozens of BoKs available to you, each of which has an organization pushing for its adoption. Many of these BoKs contain a lot of "old-style thinking" that is still being presented as leading edge "industry best practices." There are some great ideas in these BoKs, don't get us wrong, but those great ideas aren't always applicable to your situation and these BoKs contain many incredibly questionable ideas. What the DA framework does is it leverages the strategies captured in these BoKs, putting them into context for you so that your teams can choose accordingly – all valuable stuff to capture in your organizational process knowledgebase. To succeed in today's hyper-competitive environments we must optimize our whole organization, and to do that we must harvest the learnings from a wide range of sources.

Table 1.1. A sampling of bodies of knowledge.

Process Area	Bodies of Knowledge (BoKs)
Business Analysis	International Institute of Business Analysis (IIBA) BoK
Data Management	Data Management Association (DAMA) Data Management BoK (DMBoK)
Development	The "Agile Canon", the Software Engineering BoK (SWEBoK), and Software Engineering Method and Theory (SEMAT)
Enterprise Architecture	The Open Group Architecture Framework (TOGAF), The Zachman Framework, the International Association of Software Architects (IASA) BoK, and the Department of Defense Architecture Framework (DODAF)
Human Operations	Human Resources Body of Knowledge (HRBoK)
IT Governance	COBIT (Control Objectives for Information and Related Technology)
Operations	Information Technology Infrastructure Library (ITIL)
Product Management	Product Management and Marketing Body of Knowledge (ProdBoK)
Project Management	Project Management Institute (PMI)'s BoK (PMBoK) and Prince2
Quality	Various specifications from International Standards Organization (ISO)

Your Improvement Journey

Given the dynamic nature of your organization, a fair question to ask is how can you support the process improvement efforts of your people? We begin with a few key observations:

1. **Improvement is a journey, not a destination**. Real improvement requires years of concerted effort, support, and guidance – not days of training, not weeks of coaching, and not (just) adoption of a new tool.

2. **Many improvement journeys start as a transformation project**. In organizations that still have a project mindset it's natural to mistakenly assume that you can simply run a short-term transformation project and "viola, you're now agile!" With a project-based approach you are likely to have many false starts until you

finally realize that improvement is a long-term proposition.

3. **Every journey is unique.** Every organization is unique, having its own challenges and its own priorities. You must tailor your approach to reflect the context of the situation that you face, one size does not fit all.

4. **Your goal isn't to be agile, it's to serve your customers better.** Many of your improvements will focus on becoming more agile or lean, but the real goal is to improve your value streams.

5. **Improvement is hard and it requires change.** If improvement were easy we'd all be perfect! Everyone, including managers and executives, must be prepared to adopt a continuous improvement mindset.

6. **Prefer a pull over a push strategy.** When change is forced on people, when you push it on them, they will resist and most likely subvert the change. Change is much more likely to stick when people identify challenges, identify potential improvements, and then willingly choose to experiment with (they pull into their process) the potential improvement(s).

7. **Your improvement efforts need to simultaneously address people (individuals and interactions), process, and tool issues.** Although you'll invest a lot more effort in helping your people, in doing so you'll find that you're simultaneously also helping them to improve their process and to evolve the tooling required to support that process. This idea overviewed in Figure 1.6. Let's work through each of the three improvement aspects in great detail.

Figure 1.6. Relative focus of improvement efforts.

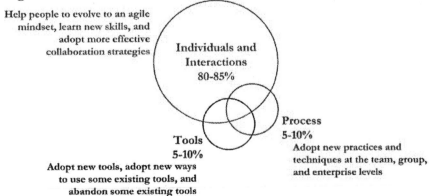

Help people to evolve to an agile mindset, learn new skills, and adopt more effective collaboration strategies

Individuals and Interactions 80-85%

Process 5-10%
Adopt new practices and techniques at the team, group, and enterprise levels

Tools 5-10%
Adopt new tools, adopt new ways to use some existing tools, and abandon some existing tools

Improving Individuals and Interactions

We have a few observations about how your improvement efforts will affect the people and culture of your organization:

1. **This requires investment in training and coaching.** People need help learning the agile and lean mindset, learning new skills required by the new practices, and learning how to use their new tools properly. This is true for practitioners, for managers, and for executives across your organization.

2. **You can't change people, they have to want to change.** If you want lasting change then people have to believe in that change, they have to want to adopt the new ways of working and thinking. They have to willingly pull changes into their environment and be given the time and resources to adapt to the changes. Otherwise when your "transformation program" ends you'll discover that people slip back into their old, preferred ways of working. Luckily, through training and coaching, people can learn how to improve themselves and their team.

3. **People need to define their own change.** When people are actively involved in identifying improvements, in working through how to implement the improvements, they "own" the change and make it theirs.

4. **People need to be happier with the new environment.** The changes need to make things better for your staff, they need to be better satisfied with the new way of working otherwise they'll be motivated to change things back to the way they were in "the good old days."

5. **Some people won't like it, and you'll need to help them.** You will find that some people are perfectly happy with the way that things are, or that they have a very different vision than the one promoted by agile and lean. At best these people will need more help to understand and accept the change over a longer period of time. At worst they will actively fight any effort to become more agile.

6. **Not everyone will survive the journey, and that's ok.** Improvement journeys prove to be perilous for some. When you begin to squeeze the bureaucracy out of your processes the people involved need to find new ways to add value to your organization. Some people are up for that, some are not. Be prepared for some people to push back and even undermine your improvement efforts – expect to have a few unpleasant conversations about your improvement strategy.

7. **Teams own their own processes**. For teams to be effective they need to be in a position to determine and evolve the way that they work. An implication of this is that everyone needs to be flexible enough to interact with other teams in a manner that makes sense to everyone involved.

Improving Your Process

We also have a few observations about how to improve your process:

1. **Recognize that "process" can be a dirty word for many people**. There are several reasons for this: Many existing processes have been pushed onto people; many existing processes are adversarial where people and teams compete for resources; many existing processes are control-based and limit access to information and resources; many processes are inflexible and ill-suited to purpose, many processes are bloated with waste, and many existing processes are coercive in nature in that they provide managers the ability to hire, fire, and punish people. Is it any wonder that many people are leery of process, and in some cases rabidly against it? It doesn't have to be this way. Disciplined agilists seek to build collaborative, flexible, and pragmatic learning processes that empower people to add value to your organization and to delight your customers.

2. **One process size does not fit all**. When every person, every team, and every organization is clearly unique and facing different situations, you must have a process framework that is flexible and easy to tailor. To do this effectively the framework must go beyond the rhetoric of "you can tailor this process to meet your needs" to actually providing real options and making their tradeoffs explicit. DA does this with its goal-driven approach.

3. **Big improvements can occur in small steps**. Small changes, particularly those that move you forward to a larger goal, are less risky, easier to implement, and easier to adopt than large "big bang" changes.

4. **Learn through experimentation**. The safest way to discover what works for you is to actually try out a new idea for a short time, observe and measure how well it works in practice, and then make a fact-based decision as to whether to continue with that change or not. Even if the experiment is a "failure" you've still learned something.

5. **Optimize the whole**. Although every organization is a complex adaptive system, and every team owns its own process, they all need to work together as a streamlined whole. For example, if your solution delivery teams are potentially able to release into production on a weekly basis but your release management team insists that they

follow a six-week deployment process then you clearly have a problem.

6. **Measure your way to success**. If you don't measure something it doesn't improve, the trick of course being that you need to measure what's truly important. Our advice is to focus on measuring improvements to value streams.

7. **Your improvement targets will evolve over time as your priorities evolve**. As you address your currently pressing challenges you will discover that new opportunities to improve will emerge.

8. **You need an organizational process knowledgebase**. Just because every team owns its own process that doesn't imply that they need to learn everything from scratch. Effective organizations enable their team's process improvement efforts by having supporting libraries of (e-)books, an evolving wiki of practices, commercial products like Enterprise Transformation Advisor from Software Development Experts, references to existing bodies of knowledge, and your corporate policies and guidance.

9. **Keep process documentation very, very light**. One of the challenges with all this talk of process improvement is that someone(s) will insist that it needs to be thoroughly documented. Ugh. Few people read process documentation and fewer yet read detailed process documentation. We strongly advise that you take an agile approach and keep your process documentation as lightweight as possible [AgileDocumentation]. One lightweight approach is to have each team define their "collaboration agreements" – sometimes called a team API, team working agreements, rules of engagement, or more formally a service level agreement (SLA). The idea is to define how others can interact with you but to keep the details of how you do so internal to the team.

Improving Your Tooling

There are several observations that we'd like to make regarding your tooling infrastructure:

1. **New ways of working will require new tools**. For software development alone you'll find that you need to adopt a wide array of new tools for testing, continuous integration, and continuous deployment. For governance you'll adopt new dashboard technologies and operational monitoring technologies.

2. **You will use some of your existing tools in new ways**. You may discover that some of your existing tools can be used in a lightweight, more agile manner.

3. **You will need to abandon some of your existing tools**. This

18

won't be clear to you at first and will likely be painful given the investment you've made in them. The strategy is to recognize these investments as the sunk costs that they are and that your real goal is to ensure that your staff has the infrastructure that they need to get the job done.

4. **You'll need to improve your physical work spaces**. This may include building work rooms so that your teams may co-locate, installing whiteboards and other collaborative tooling, and even investing in videoconferencing and smartboard technologies to support geographically distributed work.

In Chapters 7 and 8 we focus on how to successfully evolve your organization into a Disciplined Agile Enterprise.

The Final Destination: Business Agility

Business agility — an adaptive, lean, responsive, and learning organization — is the true destination of your improvement efforts [Leybourn]. Business agility is something that emerges over time through lots of hard work — there are no shortcuts, silver bullets, or process frameworks that will solve your problems. You must do the work to overcome the challenges that you face. Having said that, you don't need to go on this journey without a roadmap, nor do you need to do it alone. The Disciplined Agile (DA) framework, as described in this book, is the roadmap that will help get you to business agility. Supported by experienced, certified DA coaches your journey will be faster and less difficult.

Business agility requires true agility across all of IT, not just software development, and a Disciplined Agile Enterprise that is able to leverage that IT capability. And, because the environment in which your organization operates evolves over time, and because your competitors and partners also evolve, business agility proves to be a moving target in practice. We live in interesting times indeed!

2 BEING DISCIPLINED

If I have seen further it is by standing on the shoulders of giants – Sir Isaac Newton

What does it mean to be disciplined? To be disciplined is to do the things that you know are good for you, things that usually require hard work and perseverance. It requires discipline to regularly delight your customers. It takes discipline for teams to become awesome. It requires discipline for leaders to ensure that their people have a safe environment to work in. It takes discipline to recognize that you need to tailor your approach for the context that you face, and to evolve your approach as the situation evolves. It takes discipline to recognize that you are part of a larger organization, that you should do what's best for the enterprise and not just what's convenient for you. It requires discipline to evolve and optimize your overall workflow, and it requires discipline to realize that you have many choices regarding how you work and organize yourselves, so you should choose accordingly.

This chapter works through the seven primary principles behind the Disciplined Agile (DA) framework. These ideas aren't new, which is why we began this chapter with a quote from Newton – There is a plethora of sources from which we can adopt ideas. In fact, the DA framework has always been a hybrid of great strategies from the very beginning, with the focus being on how all of these strategies fit together in practice. The giants whose shoulders the DA framework stands on include: The 17 authors of the Agile Manifesto [Manifesto]; David Anderson for his work in Kanban [Anderson]; Chris Argyris for double-loop learning [Argyris]; Kent Beck for his work in Extreme Programming (XP), Test Driven Development (TDD), and agile software engineering in general [Beck]; Alistair Cockburn for his body of work in agile and specifically the Heart of Agile [Cockburn]; Tom DeMarco for his ideas around ensuring there is sufficient slack in your work schedule [DeMarco]; Tom Gilb for his incredible work on quality, measurement, and concurrent engineering [Gilb]; Joshua Kerievsky for sharing his experiences with Modern Agile strategies [Kerievsky]; Gene Kim for his work in the DevOps space [Kim]; Philippe Kruchten for his work on the Unified Process [Kruchten]; Frederic Laloux for his ideas around reinventing organizations [Laloux]; Evan Leybourn for his ideas and observations about business agility [Leybourn]; Mary and Tom Poppendieck for their work in lean software engineering and product management [Poppendieck]; Eric Ries for his Lean Startup strateiges[Ries]; Don Reinertsen for his work on product flow [Reinertsen]; Ken Schwaber and Jeff Sutherland for the Scrum method [SchwaberBeedle]; Dave Snowden for the Cynefin Framework [Cynefin]; And many, many others (our apologies to everyone whom we've missed).

The Principles of the Disciplined Agile Framework

The DA framework has a foundation of seven fundamental principles – Delight Customers, Be Awesome, Pragmatism, Context Counts, Choice is Good, Optimize Flow, and Enterprise Awareness. These principles are captured in Figure 2.1. Let's explore each one.

Figure 2.1. The primary principles of Disciplined Agile.

Principle: Delight Customers

For a value stream to succeed the delight of your customers must be your key priority. In 2001 the writers of the Agile Manifesto told us that "Our highest priority is to satisfy the customer through early and continuous delivery of valuable software." This is a good start, but disciplined agilists prefer the lean philosophy that to succeed it isn't sufficient to simply satisfy the customer but instead we must regularly delight them if we wish to keep them as a customer.

We delight our customers when our products and services not only fulfill their needs and expectations but surpass them. Consider the last time you checked into a hotel. If you're lucky there was no line, your room was available, and there was nothing wrong with it when you got there. You were likely satisfied with the service but that's about it. Now imagine that you were greeted by name by the concierge when you arrived, that your favorite snack was waiting for you in the room, and that you received a complimentary upgrade to a room with a magnificent view – all without asking. This would be more than satisfying and would very likely delight you. Although the upgrade won't happen every time you check in, it's a nice touch when it does and you're likely to stick with that hotel chain because they treat you so well.

Successful organizations offer great products and services that delight their customers. Systems design tells us to build with the customer in mind, to work with them closely, to build in small increments and then seek feedback, so that we better understand what will actually delight them. As disciplined agilists we embrace change because we know that our stakeholders will change their minds as they learn what they truly want as the solution evolves. We also strive to discover what our customers want and to care for our customers – it's much easier to take care of an existing customer than it is to get a new one.

Jeff Gothelf and Josh Seiden say it best in *Sense & Respond* – "If you can make a product easier to use, reduce the time it takes a customer to complete a task, or provide the right information at the exact moment, you win."

Principle: Be Awesome

Who doesn't want to be awesome? Who doesn't want to be part of an awesome team doing awesome things while working for an awesome organization? We all want these things. Recently Josh Kerievsky has popularized the concept that modern agile teams make people awesome, and of course it isn't much of a leap that we want awesome teams and awesome organizations too. Similarly the Poppendiecks observe that sustainable advantage is gained from engaged, thinking people. Helping people to be awesome is important because, as Richard Branson of the Virgin Group says, "Take care of your employees and they'll take care of your business."

There are several things that you as an individual can do to be awesome. First and foremost, act in such a way that you earn the respect and trust of your colleagues – be reliable, be honest, be open, and treat them with respect. Second, willingly collaborate with others. Share information with them when asked, even if it is a work in progress. Offer help when it's needed and just as important reach out for help yourself. Third, be an active learner. Seek to master your craft, always being on the lookout for opportunities to experiment and learn. Go beyond your specialty and learn about the broader software process and business environment. By becoming a T-skilled "generalizing specialist" you will be able to better appreciate where others are coming from and thereby interact with them more effectively [GenSpec]. Fourth, seek to never let the team down. Yes, it will happen sometimes, and good teams understand and forgive that.

Awesome teams are built around motivated individuals who are given the environment and support required to fulfill their objectives. A 2015 study at Google found that successful teams provide psychological safety for team members, that team members are able to depend on one another, there is structure and clarity around roles and responsibilities, and people are doing work that is both meaningful and impactful to them [Google]. Awesome teams have a very good working relationship with their stakeholders, collaborating with them to ensure that what they do is what the stakeholders actually need. Finally, awesome teams are whole – they are cross functional, having the skills, resources, and authority required to be successful and team members themselves tend to be cross-functional generalizing specialists.

Awesome teams also choose to build quality in from the very beginning. Lean tells us that your process should not allow defects to occur in the first place, but when this isn't possible (yet) you should work in such a way that you do a bit of work, validate it, fix any issues that you find, and then iterate. The Agile Manifesto is clear that continuous attention to technical excellence and good design enhances agility.

As a leader, you can enable your staff to be awesome individuals working on awesome teams through providing them with the authority and resources required for them to do their jobs, by building a safe culture and environment (see next principle), and by motivating them to excel. People are motivated by being provided with the autonomy to do their work, having opportunities to master their craft, and to do something that has purpose [Pink]. What would you rather have, staff who are motivated or demotivated[2]?

---

[2] If you think happy employees are expensive, wait till you try unhappy ones!

Principle: Pragmatism (Over Purism)

People are often surprised when we suggest that mainstream methods such as Scrum and Extreme Programming (XP) are prescriptive. But they are indeed. Scrum prescribes a daily stand-up meeting (Scrum) no longer than fifteen minutes to which all team members must attend, that teams must have a retrospective at the end of each iteration (Sprint), and that team size should not be more than nine people. Extreme Programming mandates pair programming (two people sharing one keyboard) and Test-Driven Development (TDD). We are not suggesting that prescription is a bad thing, we're merely stating that it does exist. Many agilists are quite fanatical about following specific methods strictly. In fact, we have met many who say that to "do agile right" you need to have 5-9 people in a room, with the business (Product Owner) present at all times. The team should not be disturbed by people outside the team, and should be 100% dedicated to the project. However, in many established enterprises such ideal conditions rarely exist. The reality is that we have to deal with many suboptimal situations, such as distributed teams, large team sizes, outsourcing, multiple team coordination, and part-time availability of stakeholders.

The DA framework recognizes these realities and rather than saying "we can't be agile" in these situations we instead say "let's be as effective as we can be." Instead of prescribing "best practices", DA provides strategies for maximizing the benefits of agile despite certain necessary compromises being made. As such, DA is pragmatic, not purist in its guidance – DA provides guardrails helping you to make better process choices, not strict rules that may not even be applicable given the context that you face.

Principle: Context Counts

Every person is unique, with their own set of skills, preferences for workstyle, career goals, and learning styles. Every team is unique not only because it is composed of unique people but also because it faces a unique situation. Your organization is also unique, even when there are other organizations that operate in the same marketplace that you do. For example, automobile manufacturers such as Ford, Audi, and Tesla all build the same category of product yet it isn't much of a stretch to claim that they are very different companies. These observations – that people, teams, and organizations are all unique – lead us to a critical idea that your process and organizational structure must be tailored for the situation that you currently face. In other words, context counts.

When it comes to understanding the context faced by a team, our experience is that in addition to their personal preferences that their process and organizational decisions will be affected by the six factors depicted in Figure 2.2. For example, a team of eight people working in a common team room on a very complex domain problem in a life-critical regulatory situation will organize themselves differently, and will choose to follow different practices, than a team of fifty people spread out across a corporate campus on a complex problem in a non-regulatory situation. Although these two teams could be working for the same company they could choose to work in very different ways.

Figure 2.2. Tactical scaling factors faced by teams.

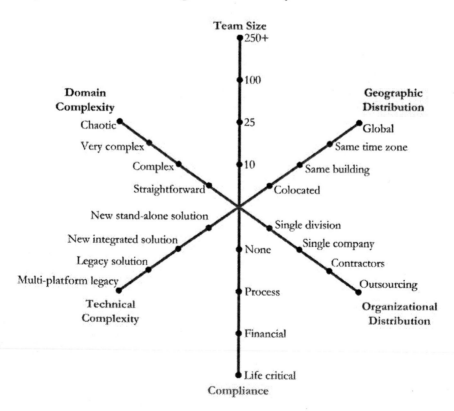

There are several interesting implications of the radar chart (also called a spider chart) in Figure 2.2. First, the further out you go on each spoke the greater the risk faced by a team. For example, it's much riskier to outsource than it is to build your own internal team. A large team is a much riskier proposition than a small team. A life-critical regulatory situation is much riskier than a financial-critical situation, which in turn is riskier than facing no regulations at all. Second, because teams in different situations will need to choose to work in a manner that is appropriate for the situation that they face, to help them tailor their approach effectively you need to give them choices. Third, anyone interacting with multiple teams needs to be flexible enough to work with each of those teams appropriately. For example, you will govern that small, co-located, life-critical team differently than the medium-sized team spread across the campus. Similarly, an Enterprise Architect who is supporting both teams will collaborate appropriately with each.

The leading agile method, Scrum, provides solid guidance for delivering value in an agile manner but it is officially described by only a sixteen page guide [ScrumGuide]. Disciplined Agile recognizes that enterprise complexities require far more guidance and thus provides a comprehensive reference framework for adapting your agile approach for your unique context in a straightforward manner. Being able to adapt your approach for your context with a variety of choices rather than standardizing on one method or framework is a good thing and we explore this further below.

Principle: Choice is Good

Let's assume for a minute that your organization has multiple teams working in a range of situations, which in fact is the norm for all but the smallest of companies. How do you define a process that applies to each and every situation that covers the range of issues faced by each team? How do you keep it up to date as each team learns and evolves their approach? The answer is that you can't, documenting such a process is exponentially expensive. But does that mean you need to inflict the same, prescriptive process on everyone? When you do that you'll inflict process dissonance on your teams, decreasing their ability to be effective and increasing the chance that they invest resources in making it look as if they're following the process when in reality they're not. Or, does this mean that you just have a "process free-for-all" and tell all your teams to figure it out on their own? Although this can work it tends to be very expensive and time consuming in practice – even with coaching each team is forced to invent or discover the practices and strategies that have been around for years, sometimes decades. Luckily, the Disciplined Agile framework provides a better way.

In Chapter 1 we showed that organizations are complex adaptive systems (CASs) where a prescriptive, "one size fits all" process will not work. The Cynefin framework [Cynefin], see Figure 2.3, shows that in a complex domain you are dealing with "unknown unknowns" and there are no right answers, just strategies that work within a given context.

Figure 2.3. The Cynefin framework.

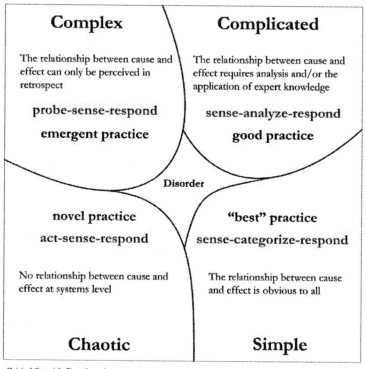

Complex

The relationship between cause and effect can only be perceived in retrospect

probe-sense-respond

emergent practice

Complicated

The relationship between cause and effect requires analysis and/or the application of expert knowledge

sense-analyze-respond

good practice

Disorder

novel practice

act-sense-respond

No relationship between cause and effect at systems level

"best" practice

sense-categorize-respond

The relationship between cause and effect is obvious to all

Chaotic

Simple

Original Copyright Dave Snowden

Let's discuss Disciplined Agile in relationship to the Cynefin framework, and in particular let's focus on IT for now. Let's explore each of the five Cynefin domains:

1. **Are you experiencing disorder?** This is when you don't know which of the other four domains that you're in. If so, gather information to determine what is happening and then start moving into one of the other domains quickly.

2. **Are you in a chaotic situation?** If your teams don't know why they are succeeding or failing you are likely in the "chaotic" domain. This is a bad place to be and you want to work your way out of that.

3. **Are you in a simple situation?** Software development is rarely "simple", and certainly not in all situations. The only exception to this is the rare circumstances where your teams are consistently building the same sort of solution in the same

sort of environments on a regular basis (likely because you're a specialized services company focused on this one thing). We've never seen this in practice, and if we did our recommendation would be to automate this work as much as possible.

4. **Are you in a complicated situation?** This is what traditional IT organizations often assume, Yes, IT is difficult but all we need to do is codify our processes in a detailed manner, train people to follow them, and everything will work out. If this was true we would have more deterministic and predictable outcomes. But this was never the case, and at best resulted in onerous processes that proved to be expensive and slow only to produce solutions that stakeholders don't really want.

5. **Are you in a complex situation?** Very likely yes, although that might not be what you want to hear. In such situations there are a large number of interacting elements (in this case people or teams) and their interactions are non-linear – minor changes in behavior can have disproportionately major consequences. These consequences emerge and evolve as the situation evolves. Luckily we *can* get more dependable results if we provide proven, situational guidance. Cynefin advises that in these situations we probe-sense-respond, often referred to "inspect and adapt". But how to adapt? Few people have a deep understanding of the vast array of potential options available. Disciplined Agile is made up of a very rich framework of process decision strategies. Yes, one could suggest that this is "complicated", but the unfortunate truth is that to try to make it "simple" is naïve. While there is a lot of content in Disciplined Agile, one does not need to understand it in its entirety. Understanding the basic structure of the DA framework and then referencing it to address complexity makes it quite consumable in practice. Of course, investing in learning as much as possible about the framework reaps dividends in efficiency.

Different contexts require different strategies – teams need to be able to own their own process and to experiment to discover what works in practice for them given the situation that they face. This is why the DA framework presents people with choices through the application of process goal diagrams, see Figure 2.4 for an example of options for addressing changing stakeholder needs throughout solution delivery (more on this in Chapter 3). The idea is to make important decision points explicit, such as when to accept changes, and then present teams with their options and the tradeoffs surrounding those options. This enables teams to make better process choices given the situation that they face. To make these choices, teams need to know: what each option is, the tradeoffs associated with each one, and in what situations the option is and isn't applicable. The DA framework takes a similar, goal/choice-driven approach to IT process areas such as Data Management and Reuse Engineering as well as enterprise process areas such as Enterprise Architecture and People Management (please see Chapters 4 and 5 for more details).

Figure 2.4. The goal diagram for Address Changing Stakeholder needs.

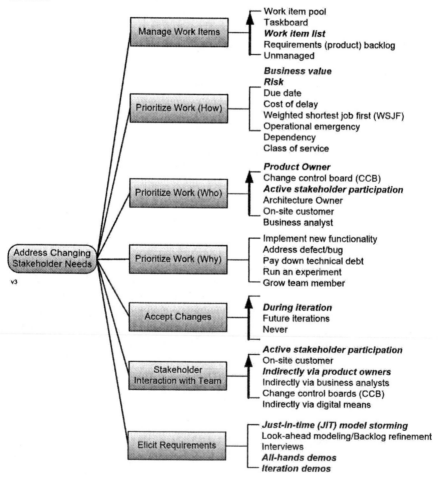

This choice-driven strategy is a middle way. At one extreme you have prescriptive methods, which have their place, such as Scrum, LeSS, and SAFe which tell you the one way to do things. Regardless of what the detractors of these methods will tell you these prescriptive strategies do in fact work quite well in some situations - as long as you find yourself in that situation they'll work well for you. However, if you're not in the situation where a prescriptive method fits then it will likely do more harm than good. At the other extreme are experimental methods such as those used at Spotify that tell you to experiment and learn as you go. This works well in practice but can be very expensive and time consuming and can lead to significant inconsistencies between teams which hampers your overall organizational process. Spotify had the luxury of evolving their process within the context of a product company, common architecture, no technical debt, and a culture that they could grow rather than change. The DA framework sits between these two extremes – by taking this process goal driven approach it provides process commonality between teams that is required at the organizational level yet provides teams with the flexibility required to tailor and evolve their internal processes to address the context of the situation that they face. Teams can choose from known strategies the likely options to then experiment with, increasing the chance that they find something that works for them in practice. At a minimum, it at least makes it clear that they have choices, that there is more than the one way described by the prescriptive methods.

There is a catchy phrase in the agile world called "fail fast" or better yet "learn fast." As described earlier leadership should encourage experimentation early in the interest of learning and improving as quickly as possible. However, we would suggest that by referencing the proven strategies in Disciplined Agile you will make better choices for your context, speeding up the learning process and failing less. Better choices lead to better outcomes, earlier.

Principle: Optimize Flow

Your organization is a complex adaptive system (CAS) of interacting teams and groups that individually evolve continuously and affect each other as they do. The challenge that we face is how do we ensure that these collaborating teams do so in such a way as to effectively implement our organization's value streams? How do we ensure that these teams are well aligned, remain well aligned, and better yet improve their alignment over time?

The implication is that as an organization we need to optimize our overall workflow. The DA framework supports a large number of strategies to do so:

1. **Deliver continuously at a sustainable pace**. The Disciplined Agile Manifesto advises teams to deliver consumable solutions frequently, from a couple of weeks to a couple of months, with a preference to the shorter time scale. This philosophy is one of four, in this case *Deliver*, promoted by the Heart of Agile [Cockburn]. Similarly it is one of four philosophies of Modern Agile, in this case *Deliver Value Continuously*, and it is a fundamental strategy of Disciplined DevOps (see Chapter 4). Since 2001 agilists have shown that it is possible to deliver high-quality systems quickly. By limiting the work of a team to its capacity, which is reflected by the team's velocity (this is the number of "points" of functionality which a team delivers each iteration), or by limiting work in progress (WIP) and measuring cycle/lead time you can establish a reliable and repeatable flow of work. An effective organization doesn't demand teams do more than they are capable of, but instead asks them to self-organize and determine what they can accomplish. Enabling these teams to delivering potentially shippable solutions on demand motivates them to stay focused on continuously adding value.

2. **Optimize the whole**. Disciplined agilists work in an "enterprise aware" manner – they realize that their team is one of many teams within their organization and as a result they should work in such a way as to do what is best for the overall organization and not just what is convenient for them. More importantly they strive to streamline the overall process, to optimize the whole as the lean canon advises us to do. This includes finding ways to reduce the overall cycle time, the total time from the beginning to the end of the process to provide value to a customer [Reinertson].

3. **Make work flow**. The 14th principle of the DA Manifesto is to visualize work to produce a smooth delivery flow and keep work-in-progress (WIP) to a minimum. This strategy enables teams to identify and then remove bottlenecks quickly and is adopted straight out of Kanban [Anderson].

4. **Eliminate waste**. The 10th principle behind the Agile Manifesto suggests that "Simplicity – the art of maximizing the amount of work not done - is essential". Similarly, Lean advocates regard any activity that does not directly add value to the finished product as waste. Waste includes time waiting

for others to get something done, creation of unnecessary work artifacts or product features, and collaboration churn resulting from crossing organizational boundaries. To reduce waste it is critical that teams be allowed to self-organize and operate in a manner that reflects the work they're trying to accomplish. It is also important to challenge where you can reduce costs, without putting quality at risk, and to not acquire more resources than you actually need.

5. **Improve continuously**. As a leader you want to promote a culture of continuous improvement, including the sharing of skills and knowledge between people and teams, within your organization. This is seen as a fundamental philosophy of agile – The 12th principle behind the Agile Manifesto is "At regular intervals, the team reflects on how to become more effective, then tunes and adjusts its behaviour accordingly" and both *Improve* and *Reflect* are principles of the Heart of Agile. A key technique that supports continuous improvement is "double-loop learning" that promotes the idea that you modify your approach based on what you learn from your experiences.

6. **Experiment to learn**. Probably the most significant impact of Eric Ries' work in Lean Startup is the popularization of the experimentation mindset, the application of fundamental concepts of the scientific method to business. This mindset can be applied to process improvement following what Ries calls a validated learning strategy. From a process point of view, the strategy is to first identify an improvement hypothesis along the lines of "We think doing X will improve Y". Second, run a short experiment by trying it out in a controlled manner, with measurements in place to see the effect of the change. Third, observe what happens to determine the efficacy of X and whether you need to evolve X and run a follow up experiment (double-loop learning). An experimentation mindset reinforces and often speeds up the strategy of continuous learning. As we pointed out earlier, to enable an experimentation mindset within your organization as a leader you must establish a safe environment where experimentation is encouraged and rewarded.

7. **Measure what counts**. When it comes to measurement, context counts. What are you hoping to improve? Quality? Time to market? Staff morale? Customer satisfaction? Combinations thereof? Every person, team, and organization has their own improvement priorities, and their own ways of

working, so they will have their own set of measures that they gather to provide insight into how they're doing and more importantly how to proceed. And these measures evolve over time as their situation and priorities evolve. The implication is that your measurement strategy must be flexible and fit for purpose, and it will vary across teams.

8. **Prefer long-lived stable teams**. A very common trend in the agile community is the movement away from projects, and the project management mindset in general[3], to long-lived teams. Such teams evolve over time, people occasionally join the team and people occasionally leave the team, but the team itself may run for years. For example, Microsoft has had a team developing and sustaining Microsoft Word since 1981 with no end in sight. By keeping teams together, the cost associated with the teams evolving into high performance teams (forming, storming, norming, performing) [Tuckman] is eliminated. For stable teams, work flows better as the team becomes a "well-oiled machine".

Principle: Enterprise Awareness

When people are enterprise aware they are motivated to consider the overall needs of their organization, to ensure that what they're doing contributes positively to the goals of the organization and not just to the suboptimal goals of their team. This is an example of the lean principle of optimizing the whole, in this case "the whole" is the organization, over local optimization at the team level.

Enterprise awareness positively changes people's behaviors in several important ways. First, they're more likely to work closely with enterprise professionals to seek their guidance. These people – such as Enterprise Architects, Product Managers, Finance professionals, Auditors, and Senior Executives – are responsible for your organizations business and technical strategies and for evolving your organizations overall vision. Second, enterprise aware people are more likely to leverage and evolve existing assets within your organization, collaborating with the people responsible for those assets (such as data, code, and proven patterns or techniques) to do so (one of the principles of the Disciplined Agile Manifesto). Third, they're more likely to adopt and follow common guidance, tailoring it

[3] It's important to note that this move away from project management in the agile community is not a move away from management but instead from the inherent risks and overhead of projects.

where need be, thereby increasing overall consistency and quality. Fourth, they're more likely to share their learnings across teams, thereby speeding up your organization's overall improvement efforts. In fact one of the process blades of the DA framework, Continuous Improvement, is focused on helping people to share learnings (see Chapter 5 for more detail). Fifth, enterprise aware people are more likely to be willing to work in a transparent manner although expect reciprocity from others.

There is the potential for negative consequences as well. Some people believe that enterprise awareness demands absolute consistency and process adherence by teams, not realizing that context counts and that every team needs to make their own process decisions (within bounds). Enterprise awareness can lead some people into a state of "analysis paralysis" – unable to make a decision because they're overwhelmed by the complexity of the organization.

The Seven Principles...And Beyond!

If there's one thing that our discussion about the seven principles should make clear is that there's a lot more to it than seven principles! Figure 2.5 expands upon the seven Disciplined Agile principles to depict the supporting ideas, or sub-principles if you will, that we discussed earlier. Of course, the more willing one is to drill down into greater detail the more outer rings we would identify in a fractal manner.

Mindset is Only the Beginning

The disciplined agile mindset provides a solid foundation from which your organization can become agile, but it is only a foundation. Too many inexperienced coaches are dumbing down agile, hoping to focus on the concepts overviewed in this chapter. It's a good start, but it doesn't get the job done in practice. It isn't sufficient to "be agile", you also need to know how to "do agile" as well. It's wonderful when someone wants to work in a collaborative, respectful manner but if they don't actually know how to do the work they're not going to get much done. Software development, where Agile began, is complex. DevOps, and Information Technology in general, is even more complex. And the overall value streams offered by your organization even more so. We need to accept the fact that we are dealing with such complexity and act accordingly. This is why following chapters overview the strategies around Disciplined Agile Delivery (DAD), then Disciplined DevOps, then Disciplined IT, and finally the Disciplined Agile Enterprise.

Figure 2.5. Principles for being disciplined.

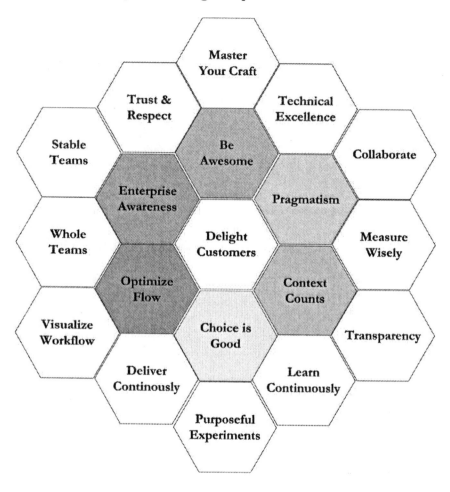

3 DISCIPLINED AGILE DELIVERY

Values and principles drive behavior. Skills and knowledge enable behavior.

Many organizations start their agile journey by adopting Scrum because it describes a good strategy for leading agile software teams. However, Scrum is only a small part of what is required to deliver sophisticated solutions to your stakeholders. Invariably, teams need to look to other methods to fill in the process gaps that Scrum purposely ignores. When looking at other methods, there is considerable overlap and conflicting terminology that can be confusing to practitioners as well as outside stakeholders. Worse yet, people don't always know where to look for advice or even know what issues they need to consider.

To address these challenges, Disciplined Agile Delivery (DAD) provides a more cohesive approach to agile solution delivery. DAD is a people-first, learning-oriented, hybrid agile approach to IT solution delivery. It supports several risk-value delivery lifecycles, is goal-driven, enterprise aware, scalable, and reflects the realities of enterprise solution delivery.

There are clearly some interesting aspects to the DAD portion of the framework. DAD is a hybrid approach that extends Scrum with proven strategies from Agile Modeling (AM), Extreme Programming (XP), Unified Process (UP), Kanban, Lean Software Development, Outside-In Development (OID) and several other methods. DAD extends the construction-focused lifecycle of Scrum to address the full, end-to-end delivery lifecycle from project initiation all the way to delivering the solution to its end users. It also supports lean, continuous delivery, and exploratory versions of the lifecycle: unlike other agile methods, DAD doesn't prescribe a single lifecycle because it recognizes that one process size does not fit all. DAD includes advice about how development, modeling, documentation, and governance strategies fit together as a streamlined whole. Instead of the prescriptive approach seen in other agile methods, including Scrum, DAD promotes what we call a "goal-driven approach". In doing so, DAD provides contextual advice regarding viable alternatives and their trade-offs, enabling you to tailor DAD to effectively address the situation in which you find yourself. By describing what works, what doesn't work, and more importantly why, DAD helps you to increase your chance of adopting strategies that will work for you.

People First: Roles in Disciplined Agile Delivery

As you see in Figure 3.1 DAD suggests a robust set of roles for agile solution delivery [DADRoles]. A common question that we get is what is the difference between primary and secondary roles? Primary roles exist in all DAD teams regardless of scale. Secondary roles, however, typically occur only at scale and sometimes only for a temporary period of time. Another common question that we get is "Why are there so many roles?" Scrum has three roles – ScrumMaster, Product Owner and Team Member – so why does DAD need ten? The key issue is one of scope. Scrum mostly focuses on leadership and change management aspects during Construction and therefore has roles that reflect this. DAD on the other hand explicitly focuses on the entire delivery lifecycle and all aspects of solution delivery, including the technical aspects that Scrum leaves out. So, with a larger scope comes more roles. For example, DAD encompasses agile architecture issues so it includes an Architecture Owner role. Scrum doesn't address architecture so it doesn't include this role.

Figure 3.1. The roles of Disciplined Agile Delivery.

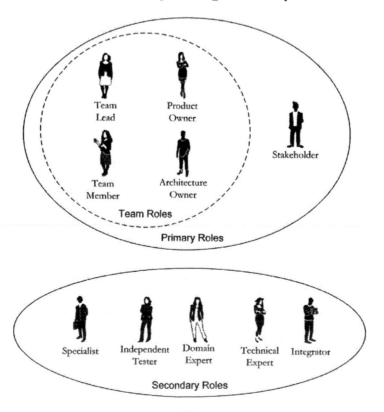

A Hybrid Framework

Disciplined Agile (DA) is a hybrid framework that builds upon the solid foundation of other methods and software process frameworks. The DAD portion of DA adopts practices and strategies from existing sources and provides advice for when and how to apply them together. In one sense, methods such as Scrum, Extreme Programming (XP), Kanban, and Agile Modeling (AM) provide the process bricks and DAD the mortar to fit the bricks together effectively as depicted in Figure 3.2.

Figure 3.2. DAD combines strategies from a range of sources.

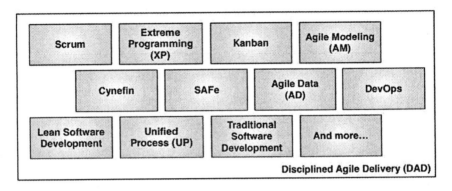

One of the great advantages of agile and lean software development is the wealth of practices, techniques and strategies available to you. This is also one of its greatest challenges because without something like the DAD framework, it's difficult to know which practices to choose and how to fit them together. Worse yet, many teams new to agile will treat a method like Scrum or SAFe as if it's a recipe, ignoring advice from other sources and thereby getting into trouble.

Choice is Good: Full Delivery Lifecycles

The focus of DAD is on delivery, although remember that other aspects of the system lifecycle still exist (these will be described in greater detail in Chapters 4 and 5). A full system/product lifecycle goes from the initial concept for the product, through delivery, to operations and support and often includes many iterations of the delivery lifecycle. Figure 3.3 depicts a high-level view of the DAD lifecycle. The inner three phases – Inception, Construction, and Transition – form the delivery portion of the lifecycle. During this portion you incrementally build an increasingly more consumable solution over time.

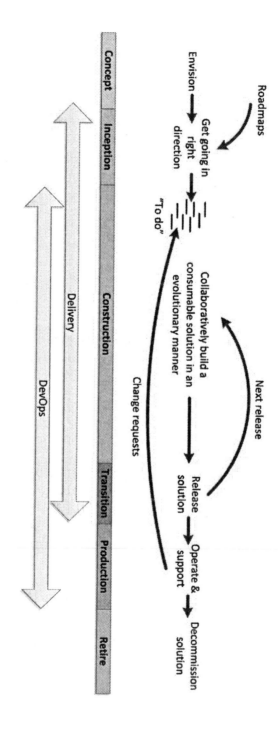

Figure 3.3. The delivery lifecycle as a subset of the system lifecycle.

Obviously there's more to DAD than what this high-level diagram shows. DAD, because it's not prescriptive and strives to reflect reality as best it can, supports several versions of a delivery lifecycle [Lifecycles]. Five versions of the lifecycle follow: an agile/basic version that extends the Scrum Construction lifecycle with proven ideas from Unified Process to support early mitigation of risk and lightweight governance; an advanced/lean lifecycle based on Kanban; an agile continuous delivery lifecycle; a lean continuous delivery lifecycle; and an exploratory lifecycle based upon a Lean Start-up approach. DAD teams will adopt the lifecycle that is most appropriate for their situation and then tailor it appropriately.

Explicit Phases Make Agile More Palatable to Management
As you can see in Figure 3.4. DAD lifecycles can have phases. Daniel Gagnon has been at the forefront of Agile practice and delivery for almost a decade in two of Canada's largest financial institutions. He had this to say about using DA as an overarching framework: "At both large financials that I have worked in I set out to demonstrate the pragmatic advantages of using DA as a "top of the house" approach. Process tailoring in large, complex organisations clearly reveals the need for a large number of context-specific implementations of the four (now five) life cycles, and DA allows for a spectrum of possibilities that no other framework accommodates. However, I call this "Structured Freedom" as all choices are still governed by DA's application of Inception, Construction, and Transition with lightweight, risk-based milestones. These phases are familiar to PMOs, which means that we aren't carrying out a frontal assault on their fortified position, but rather introducing governance change in a Lean, iterative and incremental fashion."

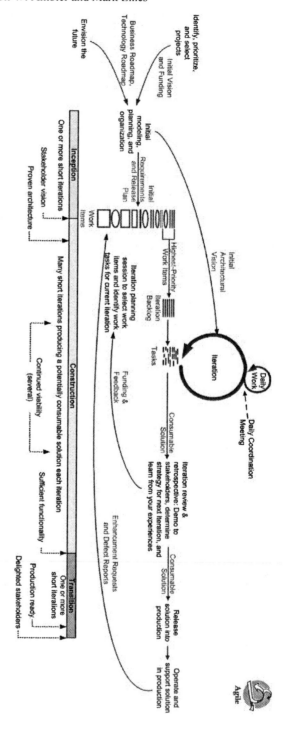

Figure 3.4. DAD's Agile/Basic lifecycle based on Scrum.

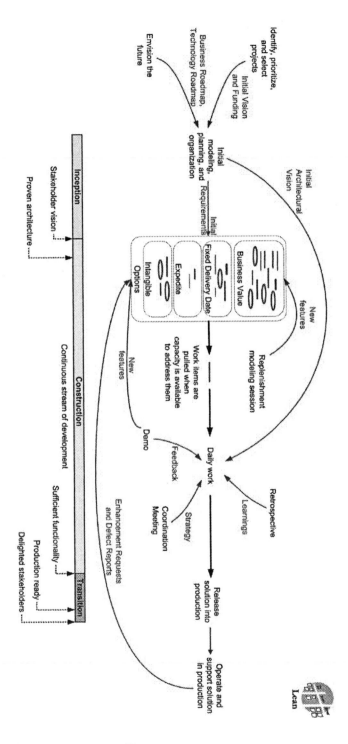

Figure 3.5. DAD's Lean/Advanced lifecycle based on Kanban.

43

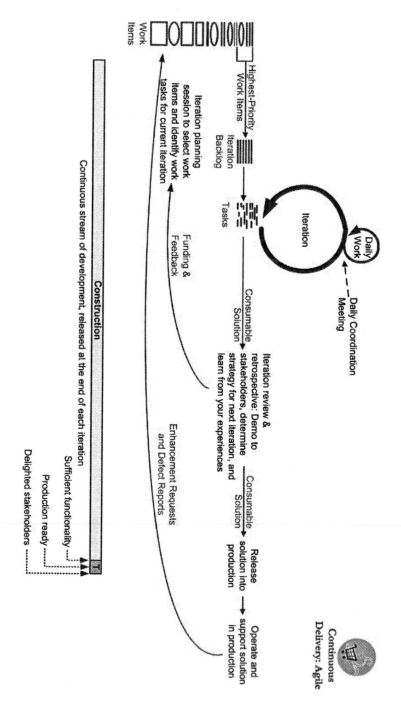

Figure 3.6. DAD's Agile Continuous Delivery lifecycle.

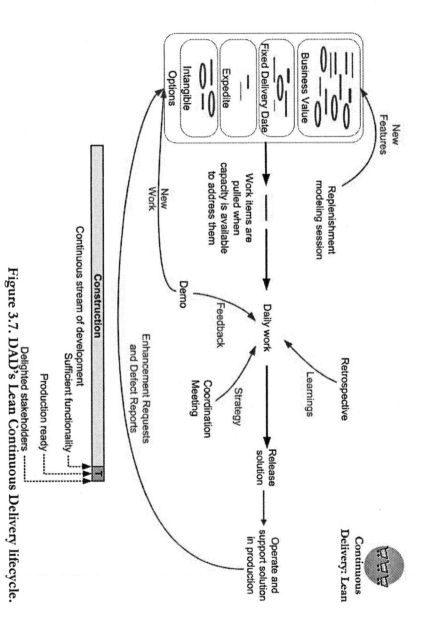

Figure 3.7. DAD's Lean Continuous Delivery lifecycle.

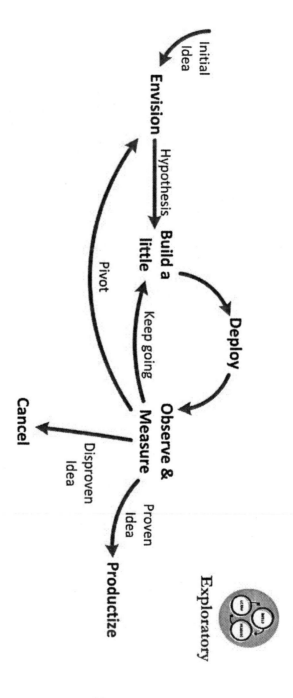

Figure 3.8. DAD's Exploratory lifecycle based on Lean Startup.

46

In general, we suggest the following guidance regarding which lifecycles fit in certain circumstances:

Agile DAD Lifecycle. This lifecycle, shown in Figure 3.4 is based largely upon Scrum and XP with a set of time boxed iterations (sprints) being the core of the Construction phase. It is the most commonly used lifecycle suitable in these types of situations:

- The work is primarily enhancements or new features
- The work can be identified, prioritized, and estimated early on
- A good choice for new agile teams
- The team is familiar with Scrum and XP
- The team is typically working on a project

Consumable Solutions over Working Software

The Agile Manifesto suggests that we measure progress based upon "working software". But what good is that if the customer can't or worse, doesn't want to use it? What we deliver should be consumable, which is *usable + desirable*. Additionally, what we produce usually is not just software. There may be business changes and other supporting deliverables. So we suggest striving to deliver "consumable solutions"

Note that while the diagram shows that you should have increments of a consumable solution at the end of each iteration, for a new product or solution you may not have something truly consumable until after having completed several iterations.

Lean DAD Lifecycle. This lifecycle, shown in Figure 3.5 promotes lean principles such as minimizing work in process, maximizing flow, a continuous stream of work (instead of fixed iterations), and reducing bottlenecks. New work is pulled from the work item pool as the team has capacity. While Scrum prescribes the use of a set of "ceremonies", such as the daily co-ordination meeting (Scrum), iteration (sprint) planning sessions, retrospectives to be done on certain cadences within the iterations (sprints), Lean does not prescribe this overhead, in fact it considers them a source of waste and instead suggests that it be done only when necessary. This requires a degree of discipline and self-awareness not usually found on teams new to agile, hence this lifecycle is considered advanced. While the concepts of Lean and the Kanban system it uses are very easy to learn, it can be difficult to master the principles of lean flow and maximizing the throughput of the system. It is suitable in these situations:

- Work can be broken down into very small work items of roughly

the same size
- Work is difficult to predict in advance. For example, teams that are focused on fixing defects or handling support issues are good candidates for this lifecycle
- The team favors the lean approach of minimizing batch size (which helps to reduce work in progress) and reducing or eliminating any planning in advance of doing the work
- The team is typically working on a series of small changes and then releasing them periodically in a manner such as a monthly release cycle

Pro Tip: Don't Pick a Scaling Framework Based On Only One Lifecycle.

Frameworks such as SAFe, Nexus, Enterprise Scrum, and LeSS are deeply vested in one lifecycle, namely Agile/Scrum. As we describe, as agile teams mature they graduate beyond Scrum to the more advanced Lean lifecycle which strips out the process waste found in Scrum (such as planning meetings, daily Scrums, retrospectives). To standardize on a Scrum-based scaling framework means that high performance lean or continuous delivery teams would actually be stepping back in their delivery capability. Companies like Barclays recognize this and have picked Disciplined Agile as their framework to allow evolution of high performance teams beyond the restrictions of Scrum and flexibility of lifecycle choice while providing the consistency of an overarching framework. Standardizing on frameworks such Nexus, LeSS, or SAFe immediately places limits on your organization's ability to maximize true business agility due to their inherent inflexibility to adapt to context and maturity. We understand that SAFe fills a need in the industry but our biggest concern is that rather than promoting moving to a combination of Lean and Exploratory approaches as advocated in the *Lean Enterprise*, it instead promotes moving from small batch Scrum iterations to large batch program increments, thereby scaling up the associated overhead with it. In our experience that is not a recipe for business agility.

Continuous Delivery: Agile DAD Lifecycle. This lifecycle, shown in Figure 3.6 is a natural progression from the Agile/Basic lifecycle. Teams typically evolve to this lifecycle from the Agile/Basic lifecycle, often adopting iteration lengths of one-week or less. The key difference between this and the Agile lifecycle is that the continuous delivery lifecycle results in a release of new functionality at the end of each iteration rather than after a set of iterations. Teams require a mature set of practices around continuous integration and continuous deployment and other DevOps strategies (see Chapter 4). This lifecycle is suitable when:

- Solutions that can be delivered to stakeholders in a frequent and incremental basis
- Work remains relatively stable within an iteration
- Organizations have streamlined deployment practices and procedures
- Getting value into the hands of stakeholders rapidly, before the entire solution is complete, is critical
- Teams have mature DevOps practices in place including continuous integration, continuous deployment, and automated regression testing
- The team is long-lived (stable), working on a series of releases over time

Continuous Delivery: Lean DAD Lifecycle. This lifecycle, shown in Figure 3.7 is a natural progression from the Advanced/Lean lifecycle. It supports the goal of delivering increments of the solution in a more frequent manner than the other lifecycles. Teams typically evolve into this lifecycle from either the Lean lifecycle or the Continuous Delivery: Agile lifecycle. It requires a mature set of practices around continuous integration and deployment in order to be practical. It also requires the technical infrastructure and advanced DevOps practices (see Chapter 4) that support this approach. It is best suited in these types of situations:

- Solutions can be delivered to stakeholders frequently and incrementally
- New work, including both new requirements and defect reports, arrives often
- Organizations with streamlined deployment practices and procedures
- Projects where getting value into the hands of stakeholders rapidly, before the entire solution is complete, is critical
- Teams with mature DevOps practices in place including; continuous integration, continuous deployment, and

automated regression testing

- The team is long-lived (stable), working on a series of releases over time

Exploratory Lifecycle. This lifecycle, shown in Figure 3.8 is based on the Lean Startup principles advocated by Eric Ries [Ries]. The philosophy is to minimize up-front investments in solutions in favor of small experiments that are market tested and measured early and often during the project. As the solution is being developed, the delivery team has the opportunity to deliver what is truly required based on feedback from actual usage. It is useful in these types of situations:

- The solution addresses high incertitude cases such as a new unexplored market or a new product
- The stakeholders and delivery team are very flexible in adapting the solution as it is being developed
- You have a valid hypothesis/strategy to test with clear go/no-go criteria for when the test is over
- You are willing to experiment and evolve your idea based on your learnings

> **Some Ideas Are Too Big For Experiments**
>
> Amazon is famous for running experiments in production to discover what customers really want. An interview with Jeff Bezos revealed that Amazon's "search inside the book" feature couldn't be run as an experiment due to requiring a critical mass of books – 120,000 apparently – to test with. Although clearly successful now, at the time it wasn't clear if people would like it and it was expensive to develop, making it a risky bet for Amazon.

In the discussion above we made it clear that teams often evolve from one lifecycle to another. This is because Disciplined Agile teams are always striving to *Optimize Flow*, to improve their process and work environment as they learn through their experiences and through purposeful experimentation. Figure 3.9 shows common evolution paths that we've seen teams go through. Along the X-axis you see that over time teams will progress towards a continuous release strategy (along the lines of Disciplined DevOps), being long-lived stable teams as opposed to short-term project teams, towards shorter feedback cycles (due to improved collaboration), and towards automated regression testing.

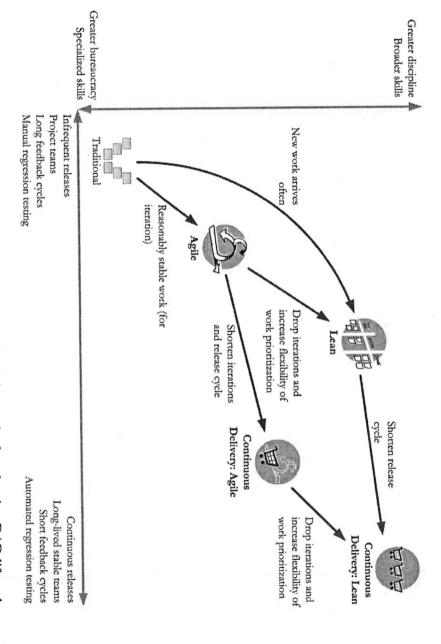

Figure 3.9. Evolution paths for adopting DAD lifecycles.

What Figure 3.9 doesn't show is how the Exploratory lifecycle fits in. This is because the Exploratory lifecycle isn't a full solution development lifecycle in its own right. It is typically used to test out a hypothesis regarding a potential marketplace offering, and when the idea has been sufficiently fleshed out and appears the product will succeed then the team shifts into one of the delivery lifecycles of Figure 3.9. In that way it replaces a good portion of the Inception phase efforts for the team. Another common scenario is that a team is in the middle of development and realizes that they have a new idea for a major feature that needs to be better explored before investing serious development effort into it. So the team will shift into the Exploratory lifecycle for as long as it takes to either flesh out the feature idea or to disprove its market viability.

Context Counts: Disciplined Agile Teams are Goal-Driven

DAD's goal-driven approach enables DAD teams to avoid being prescriptive and thereby be more flexible and easier to scale than other agile methods. For example, where Scrum prescribes a value-driven Product Backlog approach to managing requirements, DAD instead says that during construction you have the goal of addressing changing stakeholder needs. DAD then indicates that there are several issues surrounding that goal that you need to consider, and there are several techniques/practices that you should consider adopting to do so. DAD goes further and describes the advantages and disadvantages of each technique and in what situations it is best suited. Yes, Scrum's Product Backlog approach is one way to address changing stakeholder needs but it isn't the only option nor is it the best option in many situations.

In the first DAD book [AmblerLines2012], we described goals in a non-visual manner using tables that explored the advantages and disadvantages of the techniques associated with an issue. In the second half of 2012 we began expanding on this approach and developed a way to represent goals in a visual manner using what we call a process goal diagram [Goals].

Let's work through an example. Figure 3.10 depicts the goal diagram for *Explore Initial Scope*, a goal that you should address at the beginning of a project during the Inception phase (remember, DAD promotes a full delivery lifecycle, not just a construction lifecycle). Where some agile methods will simply advise you to populate your product backlog with some initial user stories, the goal diagram makes it clear that you might want to be a bit more sophisticated in your approach. What level of detail should you capture, if any (a light specification approach of writing up some index cards and a few whiteboard sketches is just one option you should consider)? How are you going to explore potential usage of the system? Or the UI requirements? Or the business process(es) supported by the solution? Default techniques, or perhaps more accurately suggested starting points, are shown in bold italics. Notice how we suggest that you likely want to default to capturing usage in some way, basic domain concepts (for example, via a high-level conceptual diagram) in some way, and non-functional requirements in some way. There are different strategies you may want to consider for modeling. You should also start thinking about your approach to managing your work. In DAD, we make it clear that agile teams do more than just implement new requirements, hence our recommendation to default to a work item list over Scrum's simplistic Requirements (Product) Backlog strategy. Work items may include new requirements to be implemented, defects to be fixed, training workshops, reviews of other teams' work, and so on. These are all things that need to be sized, prioritized, and planned for. Finally, the goal diagram makes it clear that when you're exploring the initial scope of your effort that you should capture non-functional requirements – such as reliability, availability, and security requirements (among many) – in some manner.

There are several fundamental advantages to taking a goal-driven approach to agile solution delivery:

- It provides a concise, shared pathway to leaner, less wasteful process decisions.
- It supports process tailoring by making process decisions explicit.
- It enables effective scaling by guiding you through tailoring your strategy to reflect the realities of your scaling factors.
- It makes your process options very clear and thereby makes it easier to identify the appropriate strategy for the situation you find yourself in.
- It takes the guesswork out of extending agile methods and thereby enables you to focus on your actual job, which is to provide value to your stakeholders.
- It makes it clear what risks you're taking and thus enables you to increase the likelihood of success.
- It hints at an agile maturity model (this may not be a benefit).

Figure 3.10. The goal diagram for Explore Initial Scope.

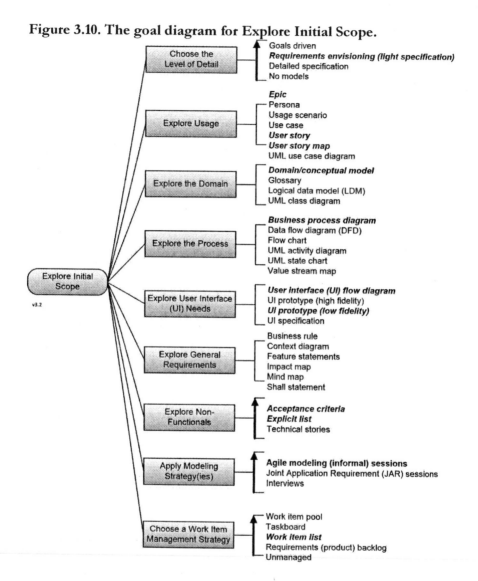

The mind map of Figure 3.11 summarizes the goals of DAD grouped by the three phases of Inception, Construction, and Transition, as well as the goals that are ongoing throughout the lifecycle.

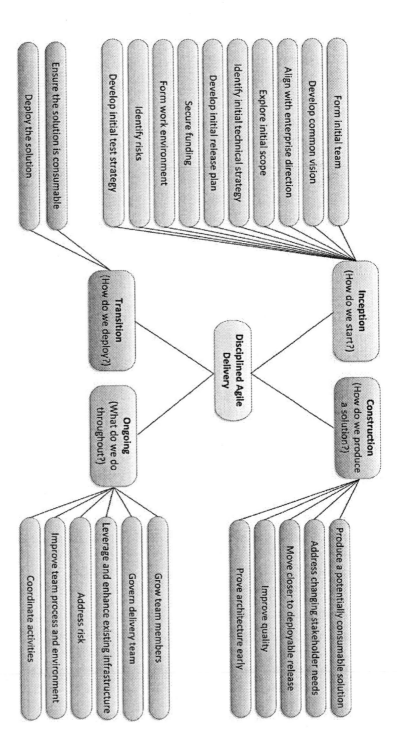

Figure 3.11. The process goals of Disciplined Agile Delivery (DAD).

But This is so Complex!

Our strategy with the DA framework is to explicitly recognize that software development (and IT, and organizations in general) are inherently complex. DA doesn't try to dumb things down into a handful of "best practices." Instead, DA explicitly communicates the complexity that you face, the options that you have, and the tradeoffs that you're making and simplify the process of choosing the right strategies that meet your needs.

So yes, there is a lot of process goals (23 in fact) depicted in Figure 3.11. Which would you take out? We've seen teams not address risk mitigation in any way, thereby ignoring the two goals Identify Risks and Address Risks, but that invariably went poorly for them. We've also seen teams choose not to address the goal Improve Quality, only to watch their technical debt increase over time. The point is that you can't safely choose to ignore any of these goals in practice. Yes, it's daunting that there is so much to take into account to be successful at solution delivery long term, but what we've captured appears to be a minimal set.

DAD Provides The Foundation for Scaling Agile Tactically

The Disciplined Agile (DA) framework distinguishes between two types of "agility at scale":

1. **Tactical agility at scale**. This is the application of agile and lean strategies on individual Disciplined Agile Delivery (DAD) teams. The goal is to apply agile deeply to address all of the complexities, what we call scaling factors, appropriately.
2. **Strategic agility at scale**. This is the application of agile and lean strategies broadly across your entire organization. From an IT point of view this includes Disciplined DevOps (Chapter 4) and Disciplined Agile IT (Chapter 5) in general. From an enterprise point of view this includes all divisions and teams within your organization, not just your IT department (the topic of Chapter 6).

Let's examine what it means to tactically scale agile. When many people hear "scaling" they often think about large teams that may be geographically distributed in some way. This clearly happens, and people are clearly succeeding at applying agile in these sorts of situations, but there's often more to scaling than this. Organizations are also applying agile in compliance situations, either regulatory compliance that is imposed upon them or self-selected compliance (such as CMMI, ISO, and ITIL). They are also applying agile to a range of problem and solution complexities, and even when multiple organizations are involved (as in outsourcing). Figure 3.12 summarizes the potential tactical scaling factors that you need to consider when tailoring your agile strategy.

Figure 3.12. Tactical scaling factors.

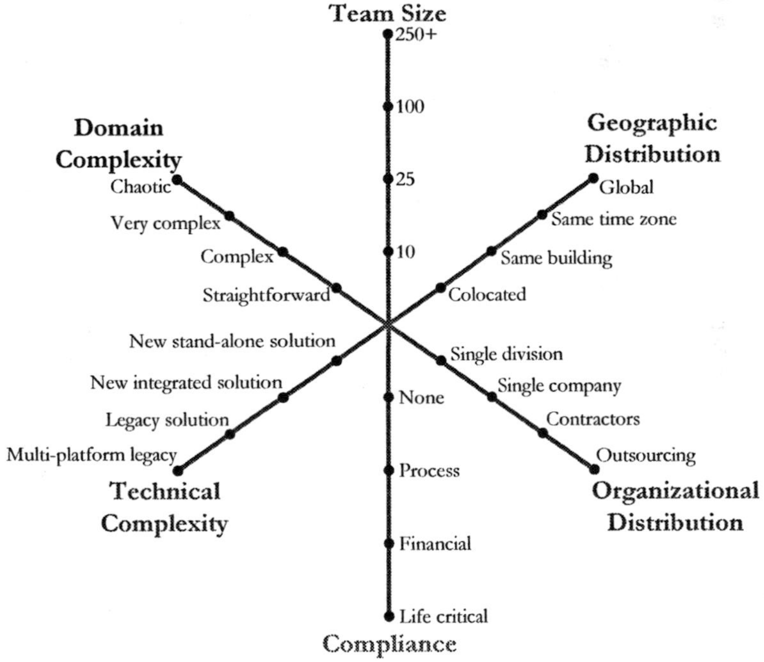

The DAD framework provides a better foundation for tactically scaling agile in several ways:

- DAD promotes a risk-value lifecycle - attacking the riskier work early in an endeavor in order to help eliminate some or all of the risk, thereby increasing the chance of success. Some people like to refer to this as an aspect of "failing fast" although we like to put it in terms of learning fast or better yet succeeding early.

- DAD promotes self-organization enhanced with effective governance based on the observation that agile teams work within the scope and constraints of a larger, organizational ecosystem. As a result, DAD recommends that you adopt an effective governance strategy that guides and enables agile teams.

- DAD promotes the delivery of consumable solutions over just the construction of working software. In addition to producing software, DAD teams also create supporting documentation, they need to upgrade and/or redeploy the hardware the software runs on, they potentially change the business process around the usage of the system, and may even motivate changes to the organization structure of the people using the system.

- DAD promotes enterprise awareness over team awareness (this is a fundamental principle of the DA framework).
- DAD is context-sensitive and goal driven, not prescriptive (remember, *Choice is Good*). One process size does not fit all, and effective teams tailor their strategy to reflect the situation in which they find themselves.

Program Management for Large Agile Teams

 An IT program is a large IT delivery team composed of two or more sub-teams. The purpose of Program Management is to coordinate the efforts of the sub-teams to ensure they work together effectively towards the common goal of producing a consumable solution for their stakeholders. In some ways "program coordination" is a more accurate term than "program management." But program management is a far more common term within the IT community so we have decided to stick with it.

There are several reasons why you may need Program Management:

1. **Some efforts are inherently big.** Many within the agile community recommend that teams remain small, between five and nine people in size, to reduce risk and overhead. But the reality is that many problems cannot be addressed by teams that small, and in fact roughly half of agile teams are ten people or more in size and one quarter twenty or more people in size [AoS2016].

2. **Overly specialized staff promote larger teams.** When you build teams of specialists (one person is focused on analysis, another on design, some on programming, ...) you end up needing more people in order to be whole. Of course, when people are more T-skilled (what we call generalizing specialists) you need fewer people in order to form a whole team.

3. **Overly bureaucratic processes promote larger teams.** You may have large teams simply because of the management and governance overhead your organization inflicts upon them. When

you *Optimize Flow* you often find that you can reduce the size of your teams or better yet get more done with the same number of people.

4. **Working on large teams can lead to greater rewards**. In many organizations the path to senior leadership is to be involved with, or better yet manage, a large program. When this is the case some people are motivated to create large programs regardless of whether it makes sense to do so.

There are several key aspects of the Program Management process blade:

1. **Coordination of a team of (sub)teams**. As you can see in Figure 3.13, there are effectively three lines of coordination required: People coordination (via Team Leads), technical coordination (via Architecture Owners), and requirements/work coordination (via Product Owners) [LargeTeams]. Each of these three groups of people will self-organize and collaborate as needed in order to coordinate their aspects of the overall program.

2. **Coordinate allocation of work between subteams**. The Product Owners will coordinate the assignment of work to the subteams and ensure that the work is prioritized appropriately. Within a large program taking functional dependencies into account when prioritizing work becomes more important to ensure that you can release working functionality frequently.

3. **Coordinate the evolution of the solution architecture**. Architectural issues, including resolution of technical dependencies and evolution of interfaces, will be coordinated through regular collaboration of the Architecture Owners.

4. **Plan the program**. The creation of the overall schedule and cost estimate (if needed) for the program is typically lead by the Program Manager. Furthermore, Program Managers often work closely with the Product Owners and key business stakeholders to perform reality checks regarding what is actually possible for the program to deliver given any schedule and cost restraints.

5. **Govern the program**. Given the greater risk involved with large programs you will want to keep an eye on value delivery, quality, team morale, and delivery schedule.

Figure 3.13. Organizing a large agile team (program).

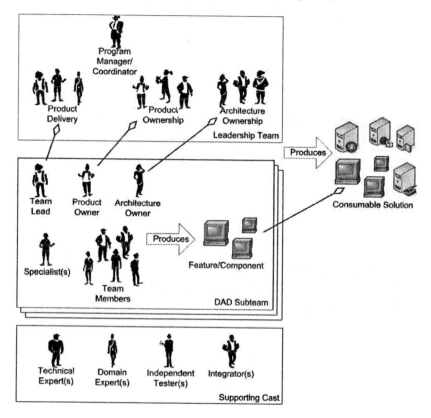

In Summary

Disciplined Agile Delivery (DAD) provides a pragmatic approach for addressing the unique situations in which teams find themselves. DAD explicitly addresses the issues faced by enterprise agile teams that many agile methodologies prefer to gloss over. This includes how to successfully initiate agile teams in a streamlined manner, how architecture fits into the agile lifecycle, how to address documentation effectively, how to address quality issues in an enterprise environment, how agile analysis techniques are applied in practice, and many more.

In short, DAD does the "heavy lifting" when it comes to the agile solution delivery process. With prescriptive methods you often have to do that heavy lifting yourself, which is time consuming and expensive. With DAD you get a leg up on how to address the issues that you face in practice in a coherent streamlined whole.

4 DISCIPLINED DEVOPS

Good news, bad news: The "good news" is that many organizations are succeeding with DevOps; The "bad news" is that DevOps takes many years to truly achieve. Unfortunately there is no agreed-to definition of what DevOps is and there is a lot of confusion over what it means in practice. In part this is because of context – every organization is unique and therefore needs to tailor their own DevOps solution – and in part because the industry is still figuring it out. Don't worry, this chapter cuts through the confusion to describe an enterprise-ready, disciplined approach to DevOps.

Defining DevOps

A common definition is *"DevOps is the streamlining of the activities surrounding IT solution development (dev) and IT operations (ops)."* In organizations that have not yet adopted a DevOps mindset we say that there is a "DevOps gap," as we depict in Figure 4.1 below. This gap results in lengthy solution deployments and hence higher costs to deploy; a long mean time between deployments (MTBD) which is often measured in terms of months; reduced market competitiveness; and reduced ability to govern your IT efforts due to lack of real-time intelligence.

Figure 4.1. The DevOps gap.

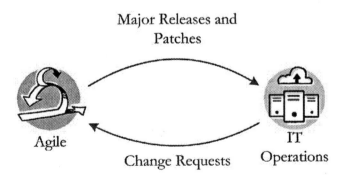

Major Releases and Patches

Agile

Change Requests

IT Operations

When organizations address these challenges by removing the barriers that inhibit effective collaboration, they close the DevOps gap. A common depiction of this strategy, sometimes called the "DevOps loop" is shown in Figure 4.2. Organizations do this by: adopting a mindset that promotes collaborative; learning-centric ways of working that are supported by agile practices; and very often investing significantly in automation. On the development side they tend to adopt a continuous delivery (CD) approach and their operations efforts become streamlined and more automated.

Figure 4.2. A closed DevOps gap.

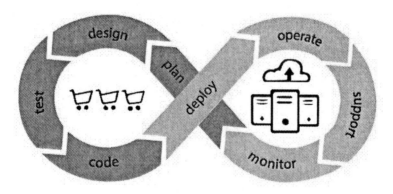

Figure 4.2 is a good start, as an initial definition of DevOps, but as an industry we are nowhere near agreement as to what DevOps really is, and there are several complimentary visions. Let's work through these visions one at a time so as to build to a coherent vision for Disciplined DevOps that addresses the challenges faced by modern organizations.

First and foremost, a key improvement over the basic DevOps vision is to explicitly bring your customers into the picture. This is commonly referred to as "BizDevOps" (or BusDevOps) and its workflow is depicted in Figure 4.3. There are two important differences in this diagram:

1. First, we're clear that DevOps isn't just for teams following an agile or continuous delivery lifecycle but is potentially applicable to any team following a lifecycle that supports incremental delivery. Having said that, a continuous delivery approach to development is certainly preferred.

2. Second, the workflow includes Business Operations which are the activities of delivering products and services to your organization's customers. There is little value in having a responsive IT organization if the rest of your enterprise isn't able to take advantage of it. BizDevOps seeks to streamline the entire value stream, not just the IT portion of it.

Figure 4.3. The workflow of "BizDevOps".

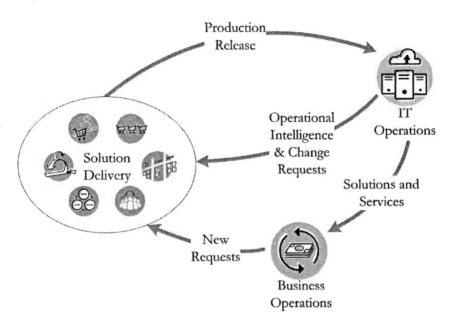

Now let's go in a different direction. Another common improvement over the basic DevOps vision is something called DevSecOps, the workflow for which is overviewed in Figure 4.4. The goal of DevSecOps is to ensure data security through improving the awareness and understanding of security issues, by adopting proactive security practices, and by incrementally identifying and addressing the most urgent security gaps [DevSecOps]. Security strategies that support DevOps include collaborative security engineers, exploit testing, real-time security monitoring, and building "rugged software" that has built-in security controls. In some ways security and DevOps have competing goals – Security wants to keep everything safe where DevOps wants to enable quick, responsive changes to the marketplace. Ensuring safety will slow things down yet being responsive increases the chance of inadvertently introducing security holes. Because DevOps will never be a replacement for formal security practices it is important to find a viable middle ground as provided by DevSecOps.

Figure 4.4. The workflow of "DevSecOps".

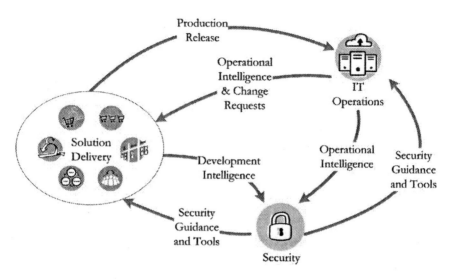

Similarly, Data Management is often missing from the DevOps picture. To our knowledge no one has coined the term "DevDataOps" so we'll do so for the sake of expediency. The goal of DevDataOps is to ensure a fair balance between the competing needs of data management in that it wants to provide timely and accurate information to your organization and DevOps in wanting to be responsive to the marketplace. Where DevSecOps is a safety vs flexibility tradeoff, DevDataOps is an accuracy vs. flexibility issue. The DevDataOps workflow is depicted in Figure 4.5. Supporting data management activities includes: the definition, support, and evolution of data and information standards and guidelines; the creation, support, evolution, and operation of data sources of record within your organization; and the creation, support, evolution, and operation of data warehouse (DW)/business intelligence (BI) solutions.

Figure 4.5. The workflow of "DevDataOps".

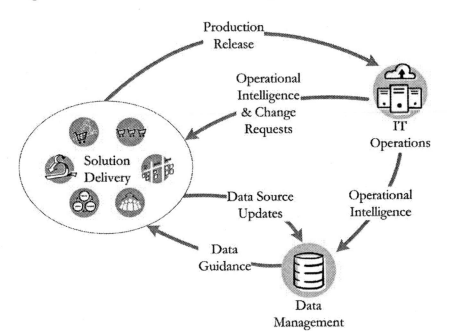

Let's consider a third viewpoint to extending DevOps. Some people choose to include Release Management and Support (help desk) activities in with the IT Operations efforts. Although this is a perfectly fine decision, our experience is that in doing so you risk downplaying these important activities. Furthermore, in large organizations Release Management can become a critical activity – When you have a handful of delivery teams coordinating their releases, it is straightforward. But, when there are dozens or even hundreds of solution delivery teams working in parallel it can be very challenging to ensure that their releases go smoothly. In Figure 4.6 we explicitly call out Release Management, IT Operations, and Support to make the workflow clear.

Figure 4.6. The workflow of DevOps with Release Management and Support.

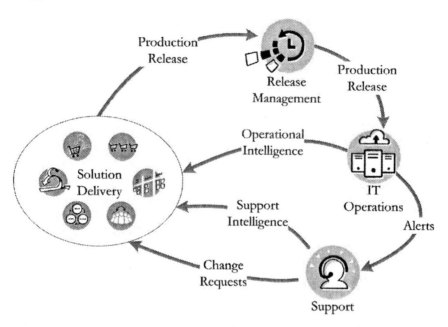

We're now in a position to understand what a Disciplined DevOps strategy actually entails. Figure 4.7 depicts the workflow of Disciplined DevOps, which is a combination of the workflows of Figures 4.3 through 4.6. Our point is that the BusDevOps, DevSecOps, and DevDataOps strategies all have their merits as does the strategy of making Release Management, Support, and IT Operations explicit. As the result of this thinking, we propose the following definition: *Disciplined DevOps is the streamlining of IT solution development and IT operations activities, along with supporting enterprise-IT activities such as Release Management, Support, Security and Data Management, to provide more effective outcomes to an organization.*

Figure 4.7. The full workflow of Disciplined DevOps.

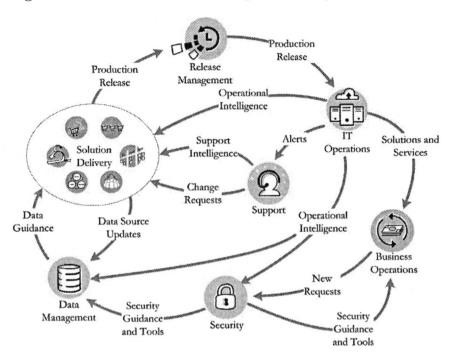

Why Disciplined DevOps?

There are many reasons that your organization should be serious about adopting a Disciplined DevOps approach:

1. **Faster time from concept to cash.** DevOps shortens the timeline from when an idea is generated by someone to the point in time it is implemented and running in production generating revenue. This occurs due to streamlined work, better collaboration, and improved decision making due to shortened feedback cycles.

2. **Improved market competitiveness.** Organizations with Disciplined DevOps strategies in place tend to be more responsive and competitive in their marketspaces. This is the result of DevOps strategies such as split testing and real-time operational usage metrics, faster time from concept to cash (see above), and agile's increased collaboration with stakeholders.

3. **Improved customer service.** This is the result of better quality systems being developed to begin with and when appropriate more knowledgeable support being provided by the development

team itself.

4. **Increased dependability**. Solutions are more dependable because of their resilient architectures, automatic recovery/failover that deals with problems before end users are even aware of them, and real-time operational monitoring that alerts support engineers to potential problems.

5. **Increased staff retention**. Teams working in a Disciplined DevOps manner have team members with increased skills and better morale. There are also more opportunities to learn and to visibly add value in such environments.

6. **Improved governance**. Disciplined DevOps provides greater visibility from IT intelligence (automated dashboard) strategies and shorter feedback cycles. Greater visibility in turn leads to more informed decision making and better control.

7. **Lower cost**. Disciplined DevOps also leads to lower IT costs through increased automation and decreased bureaucracy.

To succeed at Disciplined DevOps you need a new mindset; new processes and practices; and new tools. We explore these topics in the following sections.

The Disciplined DevOps Mindset

There are several key aspects to the Disciplined DevOps mindset:

1. **One team**. An important aspect of the DevOps mindset is shifting away from a "them versus us mindset" to an "us mindset." We all work together as a single, streamlined collaborative team.

2. **You build it, you run it**. An extreme form of the one team concept is the "you build it you run it" philosophy (or more accurately "you build it, you deploy it, you run it, you enhance it, you support it") where there are no separate development, operations, data administration teams but instead there are long-running product teams who are responsible for the entire lifecycle of a product. Having said that, larger organizations will still have operations teams responsible for supporting common infrastructure and services (e.g. your call center).

3. **Cross-functionality**. Effective delivery teams are cross-functional and made up of cross-functional, T-skilled "generalizing specialists." A generalizing specialist has one or more specialties (enabling them to add value), at least a general understanding of the overall process and business domain (enabling them to collaborate effectively), and a desire to gain more knowledge and skills. To build up such teams requires an

investment in training, education, and coaching over a long period of time - most people will require many months, and sometimes years, to become generalizing specialists. With agile, delivery team members needed skills across the entire delivery lifecycle (such as analysis skills, testing skills, programming skills, and so on). However, with DevOps, IT professionals now also need skills through the entire systems lifecycle, including delivery skills as well as production skills (operations, support, security, and so on).

4. **Architecting for resilience**. A DevOps mindset changes the way you architect your solutions. When you are expected to keep your system running, then you will invest some thought into ensuring that you can detect problems with the system and automatically take action to avoid outages. Architecting your solution to isolate change and have duplicate production instances with automatic failover minimizes the risk of outages. Resilient "DevOps-friendly" architectures permit companies like Amazon to achieve an 11-second mean time between deployed changes. We discuss architecture strategies in more detail later in this chapter.

5. **Transparency**. In general agile strategies provide significantly greater transparency than older, waterfall strategies through continuous collaboration, information radiators, and automated dashboards. Automated dashboards, an application of business intelligence (BI) strategies that the DA framework refers to as development intelligence, have become the norm for agile solution delivery. Disciplined DevOps takes this further by applying the same strategy to transparently provide operational intelligence that offers real-time insights into what is happening in production. We say that "IT intelligence" is the combination of development intelligence and operational intelligence. This IT intelligence enables: teams to self-organize more effectively because they can make informed, fact-based decisions; senior IT management to govern more effectively given the greater transparency; and business management greater insight into the effectiveness of their IT investment.

6. **Continuous improvement**. Disciplined agilists strive to learn from their experiences as well as from others so that they can continuously improve the way that they work together, including how they approach DevOps.

7. **Learn through experimentation**. Teams must be free to experiment, to try new strategies to discover what works for them in the situations that they face. Very often these experiments will

work out well, with a few stumbles along the way, but every so often the experiment will show that the strategy just isn't right for this team. That should still be considered a successful experiment, learning what doesn't work is just as valuable as learning what does, and the team should not be worried about recrimination for "failed" experiments. Eric Ries calls this approach "validated learning."

8. **Continuously streamline your workflow.** Organizations are complex adaptive systems, with thousands of "moving parts" that evolve on a daily basis. As a result we must continuously visualize and examine the way that we work so as to identify bottlenecks and potential opportunities for improvement.

9. **Optimize the whole.** We must strive to improve flow through the entire organizational ecosystem, not just locally optimize pieces of it. What good is a "perfect" data management process if it proves to be a bottleneck to teams hoping to release changes into production? What good is a hyper-efficient solution delivery process if it produces silo solutions that don't take advantage of existing resources or even work well together? Our teams must collaborate effectively as a whole, and that implies everyone must be enterprise aware and choose to optimize the overall process instead of simply locally optimizing their own strategies.

10. **Automate, automate, automate.** Most DevOps practices are enabled through automation. This includes, but is not limited to, automated regression testing, continuous integration (CI), continuous deployment (CD), operational monitoring, automated dashboards, and many more areas. Organizations that are successful at DevOps continuously look for ways to automate as much of their workflow as possible so as to free up people to focus on value added work.

11. **Eliminate technical debt.** The higher the quality of something the easier it is to understand, the easier it is to work with and evolve, and the easier (and cheaper) it is to operate. The elimination of technical debt is a short term investment for long-term gain.

12. **Reuse good stuff.** Reuse enables DevOps for several reasons. First, reusable assets tend to be of high quality (and when they are not they are soon refactored to be so) which means they are easier to work with and evolve. Second, the more you can reuse the less you need to build, speeding up development. Third, the greater the level of reuse within an organization the easier it is to deploy common changes because you have less to update.

Fourth, the more things are reused the fewer things need to be operated and supported in production, reducing the overall overhead of doing so.

Disciplined DevOps Strategies

An important philosophy of the Disciplined Agile (DA) framework is to provide people with explicit choices and to describe the tradeoffs associated with those choices. However, for the sake of brevity, in this chapter we're going to focus on what we feel to be the most appropriate choices to support an effective Disciplined DevOps approach[4]. Let's explore several categories:

- Solution Delivery
- Operations
- Support
- Release Management
- Data management
- Security

There are several development strategies that support Disciplined DevOps that you may wish to adopt:

1. **Integrated configuration management.** Developers and operations professionals often have different views about configuration management (CM) – developers apply configuration management strategies to manage the assets that they create whereas operations apply CM strategies to manage the assets that make up the IT production infrastructure of your organization. An integrated approach to CM combines both.

2. **Integrated change management.** From a DevOps perspective, change management is the act of ensuring successful and meaningful evolution of the IT infrastructure to better support the overall organization. This is tricky enough at a team level because many technologies, and even versions of similar technologies, will be used in the development of a single solution. An integrated change management strategy considers the needs of a large number of solutions running and interacting in production simultaneously.

3. **Canary tests.** A canary test is a small experiment where new functionality is deployed to a subset of end users so you can

[4] For detailed articles visit http://DisciplinedAgileDelivery.com

71

determine whether that functionality is of interest to them and that it in fact works in production as expected.

4. **Split tests**. A split test, also known as an A/B test, is an experiment where two or more options are run in parallel so that their effectiveness can be compared.

5. **Automated regression testing**. Agile software developers strive to test as often and early as possible. As a result, automated regression testing is a common practice adopted by agile teams, which is sometimes extended to test-first approaches such as test-driven development (TDD) and behavior-driven development (BDD). The regression test suite(s) may address function testing, performance testing, system integration testing (SIT), and acceptance testing and many more categories of tests.

6. **Continuous integration**. Continuous integration (CI) is the discipline of building and validating a solution automatically whenever a file is checked into your configuration management (CM) system. Validation occurs via several strategies such as automated regression testing and even code and schema analysis. CI enables developers to develop a high-quality working solution safely in small, regular steps by providing immediate feedback on code defects.

7. **Continuous deployment**. Continuous deployment extends CI so that when your integration is successful in one sandbox your changes are automatically promoted to the next sandbox. The CI strategy running in that environment automatically integrates your solution there, and so on. Together, CI and CD are important technical enablers for having working and tested software at all times, including all changes made as recently as minutes ago.

8. **Automated dashboards**. The practice of using automated dashboards is called IT intelligence, effectively the application of business intelligence (BI) strategies for IT. There are two aspects to this, development intelligence and operational intelligence. Development intelligence requires the use of development tools that are instrumented to generate metrics whereas operational intelligence is an aspect of application monitoring. Automated dashboards provide real-time insight to both practitioners and to your organization's governance team.

There are several key IT Operations strategies that support Disciplined

DevOps:

1. **Standard infrastructure.** Software development practices, such as continuous deployment and initial architecture envisioning, are enabled by consistency within your operational infrastructure. It is much easier to architect for, deploy to, and support a handful of standard hardware configurations and consistent versions of infrastructure software (e.g. operating systems, databases, middleware, and so on).

2. **Developer-led operations (You build it ...).** As we discussed previously, a key strategy is for delivery teams to build, deploy, run, support, and enhance their solutions as much as possible given your environment.

3. **Shared operational infrastructure.** A challenge with developer-led operations, when taken to the extreme, is that you forgo opportunities for common infrastructure and tooling. So don't do that. It makes a lot of sense to have a team of operations/infrastructure engineers who are responsible for supporting and evolving your shared infrastructure.

4. **Solution monitoring.** As the name suggests, this is the practice of monitoring running solutions and applications once they are in production so as to provide operational intelligence.

5. **Deployment testing.** After something has been deployed you should run a quick set of tests to verify that the deployment was successful.

6. **Automated deployment.** Deployments should be automated to increase consistency and to enable continuous deployment. Part of your automation effort should be to support both self-recovery and self-testing as native aspects of your deployment strategy.

7. **Automated dashboards.** This is the application of data warehouse (DW)/ business intelligence (BI) solutions to provide insight into your operations and support efforts. Your operations team may have individual dashboards for each solution, they may combine information being generated by individual solutions into an integrated dashboard, and better yet share that information.

8. **Disaster planning.** Disciplined organizations will plan for operational disasters. This planning will include identification of potential problems, identification of strategies to address

those problems, and putting mechanisms in place to hopefully mitigate the disasters. Potential strategies to address these disasters include building solutions that self-test and self-recover, building redundancies into your operational infrastructure, having disaster procedures in place, and practicing those procedures in simulated disasters.

9. **Scheduled disaster simulations.** Disciplined organizations will run through disaster scenarios to verify how well their mitigation strategies work in practice.

10. **Random disaster simulations.** Very disciplined organizations will implement a service within their operational environment that causes problems such as server or service outages at random times. This is done to verify that your solutions really are able to automatically recover from problems and failing that at least operators are alerted to the problem. An example of this is the Chaos Monkey functionality in Amazon's Web Services (AWS) that injects random problems into production.

There are several Support strategies that support Disciplined DevOps you may wish to adopt:

1. **Self-serve support.** This includes providing online information, including both documentation and videos, and discussion forums to end users so that they may diagnose and solve most if not all of their issues.

2. **Support alerts.** With this strategy your solution detects serious problems affecting end users, such as a data source or a service/component being unavailable. When such an event occurs, and the solution isn't able to swiftly recover, the end user is informed of the problem and presented with a "Would you like help?" option. If yes, they are put in direct contact with an appropriate support person who then helps them in real-time. This is part of your solution's self-recovery process.

3. **Developer-led support.** This strategy has development teams performing the support services for their own solutions.

4. **Support sandboxes.** Some organizations choose to have a specific environment set up to enable support staff to simulate production problems.

There are several Release Management strategies that support Disciplined DevOps that you may wish to adopt:

1. **Continuous release availability.** With this approach delivery teams are allowed to release their solutions into production whenever they need to. This is the only strategy that truly

supports continuous delivery. To make it work a host of DevOps practices are required, such as fully automated deployment, fully automated regression testing, feature toggles, self-recovering components, and many others. Large programs may have "release trains" but you need something closer to a "release airport" that enables true continuous delivery.

2. **Release service streams**. A key tenet of the DA framework is that every team is unique, and an implication of that is that some teams will need more help than others. Teams will produce different levels of quality, they will have different amounts of automation, they will have different release cadences, and so on. As a result your release management strategy needs to be sufficiently flexible to address these different situations. One way to do so is to offer different service streams, or service levels as it were, to solution delivery teams.

3. **Shared release practices**. Although this is really a process improvement issue, it's worthwhile to point out that whoever is involved with release management should actively strive to share effective practices between teams. Sharing learnings across teams is an important aspect of *Enterprise Awareness*.

4. **Synchronized IT and business releases**. In large organizations it can be a challenge to synchronize related releases across teams, and particularly across organizational boundaries. In DevOps environments the IT delivery teams can often produce new business value before the business is ready to receive it, particularly in complex value streams where many teams are collaborating. Your release management process is often where multi-team releases are coordinated.

There are several Data Management strategies that support Disciplined DevOps you may wish to adopt:

1. **Data and information guidelines**. An easy way to promote greater consistency within data and information sources is to provide common guidance that teams will adopt and then follow. This guidance should be defined, supported, and evolved over time in a collaborative and open manner.

2. **Quality data sources**. Your production data sources, including files, databases, and data feeds, should be high quality assets that are easy to work with. When it comes to data sources of record this is particularly important, but unfortunately this is little more than fanciful thinking in many

organizations. With a Disciplined DevOps mindset teams realize that they should be very careful about increasing the technical debt within their data sources, and more importantly invest in the effort to pay down any technical debt that they find via agile database techniques such as database refactoring [DBRefactoring].

3. **IT intelligence**. IT intelligence is the creation, support, evolution, and operation of data warehouse (DW)/business intelligence (BI) solutions that support the management and governance of your IT efforts. From a Disciplined DevOps perspective, there are two important aspects of IT intelligence: development intelligence that provides insight into how delivery teams are working and operational intelligence that provides insight into what occurs in production.

There are several Security strategies that support Disciplined DevOps you may wish to adopt:

1. **Build "rugged software."** Rugged software is a recent movement in the IT industry that recognizes the need for robustness, quality and security [Rugged]. An implication of this is that software-based solutions should have appropriate security control features built in, including but not limited to access control, monitoring, validated input, and sanitized data transfers.

2. **Automated separation of duties (SoD)**. The need for regulatory compliance, particularly around security, is very common. Standards such as Payment Card Industry Data Security Standard (PCI DSS) or ISO 27001 typically require separation of duties (SoD). Although much is made of the issue that the person who develops something should be different than the person who deploys, a continuous deployment (CD) strategy where things are deployed by your tools (and appropriate logging occurs) can still pass a compliancy audit. In fact, this level of automation tends to provide better SoD control than what you find when people are involved with manually running scripts.

3. **Collaborative security engineers**. As with other enterprise IT staff – such as enterprise architects, reuse engineers, or data managers – security engineers can and should collaborate closely with the teams they support. They should actively strive to transfer their skills and knowledge whenever they can so as to enable teams to be as self-sufficient as possible.

4. **Exploit testing**. Also known as penetration testing, the goal

is to simulate common ways that attackers can exploit potential security gaps. It is common to have such testing tools as part of your continuous integration (CI) strategy.

5. **Real-time security monitoring**. Your operational systems should be monitored in real-time for potential attacks/exploits. This is an important aspect of your operational intelligence.

Architecting for DevOps

Support for DevOps must be architected into your solutions, and in fact loosely coupled and highly cohesive architecture proves to be an important enabler of DevOps in practice. For new systems this is reasonably straightforward, for existing legacy systems this will likely require investment in paying down technical debt (more on this later). These architecture efforts occur at both the solution/product level as well as the enterprise level.

There are several common DevOps-friendly features that developers with a Disciplined DevOps mindset will choose to build into their solutions:

1. **Feature access control**. To support experimentation strategies such as canary tests and split tests it must be possible to limit end user access to certain features. This strategy must be easy to configure and deploy, a common approach is to have XML-based configuration files that contain the meta-data required to drive an access control framework.

2. **Monitoring instrumentation**. Developers with a Disciplined DevOps mindset will build instrumentation functionality – logging and better yet real-time alerts – into their solutions. The purpose is to enable monitoring, in (near) real-time, of their systems when they are operating in production. This is important to: the people responsible for keeping the solution running, the people supporting the solution, the people responsible for debugging and fixing any problems, and your operational intelligence efforts. Monitoring instrumentation enables canary tests and split tests by providing the data required to determine the effectiveness of the feature or strategy under test.

3. **Feature toggles**. A feature toggle is effectively a software switch that allows you to turn features on (and off) when appropriate. A common strategy is to turn on a collection of

related functionality that provides a value stream, often described by an epic or use case, all at once when end users are ready to accept it. Feature toggles are also used to turn off individual features when it's discovered that the feature isn't performing well (perhaps the new functionality isn't found to be useful by end users, perhaps it results in lower sales, and so on). Another benefit of feature toggles is that they enable you to test and deploy functionality into production on an incremental basis.

4. **Trunk-based development.** Combined with the use of feature toggles, trunk-based development is a strategy whereby the team works off the same branch of source code as an alternative to developing on feature branches which can cause merge and integration problems. Changes in progress can be delivered into the production system but isolated from production features by hiding them behind a disabled feature. When ready the feature can be simply turned on.

5. **Self-testing**. One strategy to make a solution more robust, and thus easier to operate, is to make it self-testing. The basic idea is that each component of a solution includes basic tests to validate that it can properly run while in production. For example, an application server may run basic tests at startup such as verifying the version of the operating system or of frameworks that it relies on. While the server is running it might regularly check to see if other components that it relies on, such as data sources and middleware services, are available. When a problem is detected it minimally should be logged, better yet an alert should be posted if intervention by a person is required, and even better yet the solution should try to recover from the problem.

6. **Self-recovery**. When a system runs into a problem it should do its best to automatically recover and continue on as before. For example, if the system detects that a data source is no longer available it should try to restart that data service. If that fails, it should record change transactions where possible and then process them until the data service becomes available again. A good example of this is an ATM. When ATMs lose their connection to a bank's financial processing system they will continue on for a period of time independently. They will allow people to withdraw money from their accounts, perhaps putting a limit on the amount withdrawn to limit potential problems with overdrawn accounts. People will still be able to

deposit money but will not be able to get a current balance or see a statement of recent transactions. Self-recovery functionality provides a better experience to end users and reduces the operational burden on your organization.

There are also several Enterprise Architecture (EA) strategies that are key to supporting Disciplined DevOps:

1. **Development guidelines**. An important aspect of enterprise architecture is the development of guidance for addressing common concerns across IT delivery teams. Your organization may develop connectivity guidelines, coding standards, and many others. By following common development guidelines your IT delivery teams produce more consistent solutions which in turn makes them easier to operate and support once in production, thereby supporting your DevOps strategy.

2. **Technology roadmaps**. Your enterprise architecture efforts include the definition, support, and evolution of technical roadmaps that guide the efforts of the rest of the organization (business roadmaps, also important, are the purview of Product Management). This in turn supports the creation of a common and consistent technical infrastructure within your production environment, enabling common DevOps practices such as continuous deployment, automated start-to-finish regression testing, and operational monitoring that we discussed earlier.

3. **Collaborative architecture**. The Disciplined Agile framework promotes an evolutionary and collaborative approach to enterprise architecture where enterprise architects "roll up their sleeves" and actively engage with both delivery teams and with EA stakeholders. The goal is to guide people in architecture-related manners and to transfer architecture skills and knowledge to others. It is quite common for Enterprise Architects to take on the role of Architecture Owner (AO) on Disciplined Agile Delivery (DAD) teams.

Addressing Your DevOps Technical Debt

Earlier we discussed the importance of investing in your staff, to train and coach them in the mindset and practices of Disciplined DevOps. This is a great start, but there's also the very difficult work of building a technical infrastructure that can support the strategies described in this chapter. This proves to be challenging in many organizations because they have incurred technical debt – poor quality code, poor quality data sources, questionable architectures, insufficient (or non-existent) automated regression tests, insufficient tooling infrastructure – over the years. Technical debt inhibits your ability to evolve solutions easily and thereby be more competitive in the marketplace. There are two issues to consider here: what must you invest in to pay down your technical debt and what options do you have for going about doing so.

To pay down technical debt there are several things you must invest in:

1. **Automated regression tests**. Many of your legacy systems will prove to have insufficient automated testing in place, if any at all. For the legacy systems that you consider to be long-term assets for your organization you will want to begin investing in automated regression tests.

2. **Clean code**. Clean code is significantly easier to understand, to evolve, and to test than poor quality code. There is a clear correlation between quality and speed in the IT world – high quality enables high speed, low quality slows you down.

3. **Clean data**. Organizations need high-quality data if they are going to be able to benefit from Disciplined DevOps. Data quality has unfortunately been a significant challenge for organizations with traditional data management strategies in place, but luckily the agile community has developed a host of concrete data quality techniques to alleviate this problem [AgileData].

4. **Operational and reporting infrastructure**. Many organizations do not (yet) have the capability to support IT intelligence strategies – your solutions must be instrumented to provide the operational monitoring and logging required, you must adopt integrated dashboard technologies, and your development tools must integrate into your overall dashboard strategy.

There are several approaches, which may be combined, for paying down technical debt:

1. **Refactoring**. A refactoring is a small change, such as renaming an operation or splitting a database column, that improves the quality of your design without changing the semantics in a practical manner. An individual refactoring typically only takes a few minutes to implement. Because of this minimal cost you should strive to embed refactoring into your culture.

2. **Technical stories**. When an improvement will require several hours or even a few days to complete you should write a technical story to describe it. Technical stories are just another

type of work item for a delivery team that should be prioritized and addressed accordingly.

3. **Small projects.** When a change is fairly major, perhaps you need to rewrite an entire module or replace a framework with a better one, then you should consider treating this work like a small project. These improvement projects typically require several weeks to several months of effort to complete.

4. **Solution replacements.** Sometimes you need to replace a system outright, often with a commercial-off-the-shelf (COTS) package or even by building a new system from scratch. These are typically performed as large, high-risk projects requiring many work-years to complete.

How to Mess This Up

We see several common anti-patterns when it comes to DevOps:

1. **DevOps = Continuous Delivery.** This is a common misconception amongst developers – continuous delivery is such a huge improvement for them, and often very different than what they're used to in the past, that surely this must be what DevOps is all about. This misunderstanding unfortunately limits organizations from achieving the full benefits of a more robust approach.

2. **DevOps = Cloud.** This vision is often promoted by vendors with cloud-based products to sell you, surprisingly enough. Many of these product offerings are clearly helpful, and having someone else operate a portion of your infrastructure (whatever is in the cloud) can certainly make things easier. But a key aspect of DevOps is mindset, and that has nothing to do with "the cloud." Furthermore, many organizations have implemented very streamlined DevOps strategies with little or no cloud technologies involved. You want to adopt the most appropriate technologies, including but not limited to cloud-based ones.

3. **DevOps = Microservices.** This vision is often promoted by developers who are enamored with Microservices architectures. This is in fact a very good architectural strategy in the right situation, and is often viewed as an enabler of DevOps. BUT, as we discussed earlier, the real enabler is good architecture with Microservices being one such strategy. Furthermore, you could still have a Microservices architecture yet still have a long way to go to get to DevOps.

4. **Partial DevOps.** The movements around DevSecOps and

BusDevOps are the primary culprits of this misunderstanding, and if DevDataOps ever takes off then that will only make things worse. Although these are all great ideas, all it takes is one aspect of the actual workflow to be questionable and your DevOps strategy falls apart. Disciplined DevOps explicitly addresses all aspects of the DevOps lifecycle so as to make it clear how it all fits together.

5. **Vendor-driven DevOps**. Unfortunately the term "DevOps" has devolved into a marketing buzzword, with every product and services company hawking some sort of DevOps solution. When you examine their offerings from a Disciplined DevOps point of view you quickly see that they have a limited collection of tools and services to sell you that often does not get the job done in practice. Buyer beware!

6. **DevOps engineers**. Many organizations new to DevOps will create a position called "DevOps Engineer." The responsibilities often vary, but they usually end up being someone focused on enabling continuous delivery or someone focused on sustainment and support of your solution. Don't get us wrong, both are very important things. But, DevOps is a mindset supported by process and technology, it's not a position. At best DevOps Engineer is an interim position while you're still learning your way.

7. **Treating your DevOps transformation like a project**. Adopting a Disciplined DevOps strategy is a long-term journey, it is not a destination that you reach in a few months. No matter how effective you are you can always find ways to get better.

How to Succeed

We'd like to conclude this chapter with what we feel to be critical success factors for Disciplined DevOps:

1. **Delight your customers**. With a Disciplined DevOps approach you get valuable functionality into the hands of your customers quickly and continuously, enabling you to get feedback on which you can act to make your solutions even better.

2. **Be awesome by building a collaborative and respectful culture across your entire organization**. Our experience is that people, and the way that they work together, are the primary determinants of success when it comes to adopting a Disciplined DevOps strategy. Unfortunately, it is considerably more difficult

to bring about cultural change in an organization than it is to adopt a handful of new practices.

3. **Be pragmatic.** Focus on people, but don't forget process and tooling. DevOps is primarily a mindset, but as you've seen there is a large number of potential practices/strategies (yes, that process stuff) that you need to consider adopting. In turn these practices/strategies are supported by tooling, either existing tooling that you have in place (albeit now used in a different manner) or new tooling that you will need to adopt.

4. **Recognize that choice is good.** There are many options available to you, each of which has its advantages and disadvantages. No single approach is perfect, and no single approach works in all situations. You not only need to have choices, it's incredibly good to have choices.

5. **Tailor your approach to the context that you face.** Recognize that there is no magic recipe for Disciplined DevOps, that instead you must tailor your strategy to reflect the situation that you face in practice. Although there are similarities, the fact is that Spotify works differently than Amazon which works differently than Google which works differently than your organization because these are different companies facing different challenges with different priorities. One DevOps process does not fit all. As we like to say in Disciplined Agile, context counts.

6. **Optimize flow.** You deliver more by incrementally delivering less on a more frequent basis. You achieve this by streamlining the way you work, by removing barriers to collaboration, by automating the work wherever possible, and through experiment-driven continuous improvement. When you optimize your workflow you maximize the value delivered.

7. **Be enterprise aware.** When you only focus on a part of your overall strategy you run the risk of locally optimizing that part and thereby creating something that doesn't fit with the other parts (which also may be locally optimized). The challenge is to understand what is the "whole?" For example, Disciplined DevOps is part of Disciplined Agile IT (Chapter 5) which in turn is part of Disciplined Agile Enterprise (Chapter 6). Although our focus here has been on Disciplined DevOps, that arguably isn't the whole picture. At a minimum any improvements you make for DevOps must reflect the needs of the rest of your organization.

5 THE DISCIPLINED AGILE IT DEPARTMENT

As the name suggests Disciplined Agile Information Technology (DAIT) addresses how to apply agile and lean strategies to all aspects of IT. This includes the majority, if not all, of your IT delivery teams and the IT-level teams support activities such as enterprise architecture, operations, support (IT help desk), portfolio management, IT governance, and other topics. DAIT is one aspect of strategic agility at scale, which is the application of agile and lean strategies across your entire organization. Disciplined Agile Enterprise (DAE), the topic of Chapter 6, addresses strategic agility at scale in its entirety.

Figure 5.1 depicts the DAIT activities and their high-level work products. The icons in Figure 5.1 represent what we call process blades. Think of a process blade as a context-sensitive process area or process activity. The idea is that the people fulfilling each blade will choose from a collection of strategies, just like we saw in Chapter 3 via process goal diagrams, reflecting the situation that the team faces. Figure 5.1 shows that each process blade contributes one or more work products, assets, or guidance to your organization's overall ecosystem. Note that the diagram only shows high-level products/assets and any inputs required to produce them are implied and are coming from the ecosystem. The exact workflow between process blades varies by organization and over time – Yes, we could create a large "SAFe-like" poster overviewing one of a multitude of possible workflows, but that really wouldn't reflect the agile philosophy that teams (or organizations) should own their own process, would it? Although Data Management, Security, and Release Management are important aspects of Disciplined DevOps they are also key aspects of DAIT, hence they are also explicitly shown in Figure 5.1. Similarly, Enterprise Architecture, Continuous Improvement, Portfolio Management, and Product Management are key aspects of a DAE, the topic of Chapter 6.

It's critical to remember that the focus of a process blade is primarily process, but we do go into potential organization-structure options on occasion. You may decide to align your teams along process blades – an enterprise architecture team focuses on enterprise architecture, a data management team focuses on data management, and so on – the fact is that it's rarely this clean and even when it is, your strategy will evolve anyway. This evolution occurs as the natural result of your organization being a complex adaptive system (CAS), as we saw in Chapter 1. As teams learn they will evolve their work strategy, and because teams collaborate with one another to implement your organization's value streams the changes in one team will motivate changes in the teams that they collaborate with. However your teams choose to organize themselves, they will strive to *Be Awesome* and continually experiment, learn, and improve over time. Diagrams such as the one of Figure 5.1 enable *Enterprise Awareness* by helping teams identify where they fit into the overall organizational strategy.

Figure 5.1 includes an icon for Disciplined DevOps, the topic of Chapter 4. This icon actually encompasses a number of process blades that we learned are part of your Disciplined DevOps strategy as well as the lifecycles of Disciplined Agile Delivery (DAD) (the topic of Chapter 3). Ideally your Disciplined DevOps strategy is comprised of teams that not only build your solution, but also release, run, maintain, and support it as well. However, the reality in most enterprises is that some aspects of DevOps are delivered by support groups external to the delivery teams. For this reason we show the DevOps blades Data Management, Security, and Release Management explicitly in Figure 5.1 so that we can address how these groups can effectively work with teams in DAIT. You can also see that there are also two process blades that are IT specific, in this case Reuse Engineering and IT Governance. Finally, there are five process blades that are arguably both IT and business concerns: Enterprise Architecture, People Management, Continuous Improvement, Product Management, and Portfolio Management.

The goal of this chapter is to overview the IT-oriented process blades, exploring Disciplined Agile strategies for addressing these critical activities effectively. We go into greater detail online at DisciplinedAgileDelivery.com and frankly every single one of these topics are worthy of a book all on their own. In fact such books, and even bodies of knowledge (BoKs), do exist although they are often written from a traditional point of view. As we indicated in Chapter 1 we're firm believers in leveraging the great ideas in these BoKs, often evolving them to make them applicable in an agile environment. But we also warned against the false promises made by existing BoKs as they often promote significant bureaucracy, and they are too narrowly focused in practice. In short, we need to tread carefully.

Let's overview each of the IT process blades, including Disciplined DevOps, one at a time.

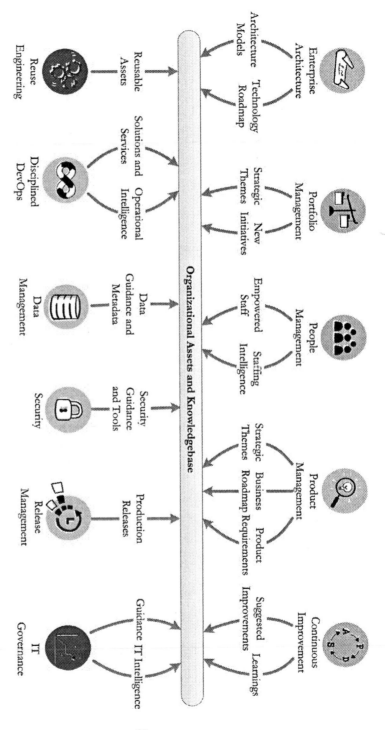

Figure 5.1 The high-level workflow of Disciplined Agile IT (DAIT).

Disciplined DevOps

Disciplined DevOps, described in Chapter 4, is the streamlining of IT solution development and IT operations activities, along with supporting enterprise-IT activities such as Security and Data Management, to provide more effective outcomes to an organization. Disciplined DevOps is a key component of DAIT and a high-level workflow for it is depicted in Figure 5.2. Disciplined DevOps encompasses several aspects:

- Solution delivery (see Chapter 3)
- IT operations
- Support
- Release management
- Security
- Data management
- Business operations (see Chapter 6)

In Chapter 4 we saw an overview of the scope of Disciplined DevOps and strategies for maximizing your DevOps effectiveness. In this chapter we take a deeper dive into each of the process blades that support and work with the DAD process for delivery teams.

Figure 5.2. The workflow of Disciplined DevOps.

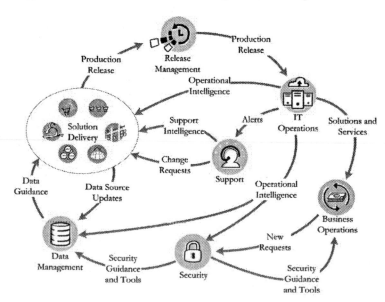

IT Operations

The primary goal of IT operations is to run a trustworthy IT ecosystem. From the point of view of your customer, you want to do such a good job that they don't even notice IT. For older organizations this can be a challenge due to the existence of hundreds, if not thousands, of legacy systems that have been deployed over the decades. You may face daunting technical debt in these systems – poor quality data, overly complex or poorly written source code, systems with inadequate automated regression tests (if any), different versions of the same system, several systems offering similar functionality, numerous technology platforms, systems and technologies for which you have insufficient expertise, and more.

As your organization transforms into a Disciplined Agile Enterprise (DAE) you will need to invest in your operational infrastructure. Much of this investment will be to pay down your technical debt and some will be to enable the operations side of DevOps. To succeed at DevOps you need systems and the infrastructure they run on to be resilient – hopefully they don't go down and when they do they recover automatically. Of course things are never 100% perfect so your operations effort will need to address disaster management and recovery as well. Smart organizations simulate disasters before they happen to ensure that their teams know how to recover when real problems arise. As mentioned in Chapter 4, disciplined companies such as Amazon and Netflix purposely simulate production problems using tools such as Chaos Monkey to ensure that their systems are resilient enough to automatically recover. When they don't their operations staff learn how to react effectively when actual problems do occur [Netflix] – this helps them to identify potential infrastructure weaknesses so as to avoid problems in the first place and to minimize the impact when bad things do occur. IT infrastructure that isn't resilient can result in significant financial loss and loss of trust by the marketplace. Consider the system outage experienced by British Airways in May 2017 where flights to and from both Heathrow and Gatwick were grounded for close to two days, the result of an engineer disconnecting and then improperly reinstating the power supply to a data center [BritishAirways]. Ensuring that sufficient documentation exists for operational systems, and supporting conventions and tooling for such documentation, is also important for long-term operational success. And of course the real-time monitoring of operational systems, and real-time reporting via your organization's IT intelligence strategy, is also important.

Successful Operations efforts balance several competing factors:

1. **Strategic (long term) versus tactical (short term)**. There is

a fine balance between ensuring operational safety while enabling the evolution of operational systems.

2. **Operations needs versus organizational needs**. You want to not only optimize the flow of operational work but do so within the context of your larger organization – *Context Counts*.

3. **Standardization versus evolution**. To reduce the overall cost and risk associated with operations, and to simultaneously make it easier for development teams to test and release changes into production, you want to standardize as much of your IT infrastructure as possible. Yet your infrastructure cannot be allowed to stagnate, it must safely evolve over time – Hence the need to work with your Enterprise Architecture efforts to envision the future and run experiments so as to learn how to evolve towards that vision.

4. **Team DevOps versus organizational efficiency**. The DevOps philosophy of "you build it, you run it" is very attractive to individual delivery teams, and it certainly makes sense for smaller organizations. But for organizations with dozens, hundreds, or even thousands of delivery teams working in parallel your costs and risks can quickly skyrocket. These organizations quickly realize that having a flexible operations/infrastructure team to support the delivery teams to leverage common infrastructure and guidance will help to optimize the overall workflow across your DAE – Follow the *Pragmatism* principle.

Support

 Your support activities, sometimes called Help Desk or End-User Support, focus on helping end users to work with the solutions produced by your delivery teams. Ideally your solutions should be designed so well that end users don't need anyone to help them but unfortunately it doesn't always work out that way. So in many ways your support strategy is your "last line of defense" in your efforts to *Delight Customers*.

There are several strategies that you should consider adopting to offer effective support to your end users:

1. **Avoid problems to begin with**. The most effective support calls are the ones that you didn't need to have in the first place. You can reduce the number of problems that people encounter through better user experience (UX) design during development

and by building a trustworthy IT infrastructure (see earlier). It is critical to recognize that any money spent on support is addressing failures as opposed to adding value.

2. **Provide self-support strategies**. With the advent of free online software such as Google Mail, Facebook, LinkedIn and more people have effectively been trained to support themselves in many cases. These techniques, such as providing online information and online discussion forums, can be employed for both customer-facing as well as internal-facing systems. Providing robust self-support options can both dramatically reduce the number of requests to your help desk and improve end user satisfaction with your solutions. A very good strategy is to post videos on YouTube describing ways to get better value out of your solutions or to address common problems that people run into.

3. **Favor proactive support over reactive**. Self-monitoring systems can now detect many problems as they occur in real-time, and often recover from those problems before your users even notice. But, in some cases it may be likely that the end user has been affected by a problem. In this case you may choose to apologize for the potential problem and ask the end user if they would like help from a support engineer.

4. **Have two-way conversations**. A key skill for anyone doing support is for them to strive to have real conversations with the end users that they're helping and not just be order takers capturing a problem description. The idea is to find out what they are trying to achieve by using your solution, to identify what is working well, what isn't, and what is potentially missing from the solution. In other words, get a sense of what end users want to accomplish so that you can better deliver value to them. Support engineers are often some of the best stakeholders for a solution delivery team because they have the most contact with actual end users and therefore will have significant insight into what they need.

5. **Solve the problem**. When end users decide to contact your support help desk the support engineer should take responsibility for the problem, explain what happened and what the process is to resolve the problem, and then see it through until the problem is resolved to the end user's satisfaction.

6. **You build it, you support it**. The DevOps philosophy of "you build it, you run it" applies to Support activities too. In small organizations, or at least those with a limited number of products,

it is common to see the delivery team itself staff the support desk for their solution.

7. **Escalate challenging problems to the team**. In large organizations you tend to need a corporate help desk that picks up the initial request and addresses the straightforward issues (typically the majority). Difficult problems will be escalated to the appropriate delivery team and dealt with by them.

Release Management

 The Release Management process blade encompasses planning, coordinating, and verifying the deployment of IT solutions into production. Release management requires collaboration by the IT delivery team(s) producing the solutions and the people responsible for your organization's operational IT infrastructure. In the case of organizations with a "you build it, you run it" DevOps mindset these people may be one and the same, although even in these situations you will often find a group of people responsible for governing the overall release management effort.

There are several reasons why you need to adopt a release management strategy within your organization:

1. **You have a complex IT ecosystem**. Many organizations have multiple technology platforms, multiple tools, and even multiple versions of a given technology within their IT ecosystem. This complexity makes it difficult for teams to safely navigate the ecosystem on their own.

2. **You have many delivery teams working in parallel**. The more teams you have working in parallel the greater the chance that they will have collisions. Lightweight coordination of your release efforts can greatly decrease the chance of collisions.

3. **Your IT delivery teams need help to release into production**. Effective organizations actively share guidelines and common deployment tooling with delivery teams. They will also provide coaching and offer to help teams setup their continuous delivery (CD) tooling and thereby help them to *Optimize Flow*.

As you can see in the goal diagram[5] of Figure 5.3 there are many strategies available to you to address release management. Where some methods such as SAFe promote one way to do this, release trains, the DA framework gives you options – remember, *Choice is Good*! You want to choose the strategies that are right for you, and when you realize that you want to improve your overall process you can use the goal diagram as an easy reference overviewing potential options. And you also need to make these process choices at the right level – Delivery teams will make decisions at the DAD level whereas a release management team (if you have one) will focus on tailoring the release management process. Disciplined Agile Enterprises (DAEs) respect their staff enough to allow them to own their process and trust them enough to know that they will make the best choices that they can.

Figure 5.3. The goal diagram for the Release Management process blade.

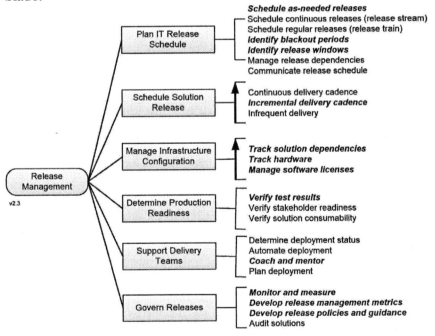

We've found that there are three key success factors for implementing

---

[5] For the sake of brevity in this chapter we're only showing one goal diagram even though each of the process blades take a goal driven approach as you're seeing for Release Management.

a Disciplined Agile approach to Release Management:

1. **Support your organization's continuous delivery (CD) infrastructure**. CD is still new to many people, and your CD tooling is impacted by the complexity of your IT ecosystem, so it makes a lot of sense to provide teams with help to learn about and setup their CD environment.

2. **Automate the determination of production readiness**. The traditional strategy to determine production readiness is to hold one or more meetings with a team to review key artifacts such as plans, test results, and deployment scripts. To support Disciplined DevOps properly these "reviews" should be automated to thereby help *Optimize Flow* through the release process.

3. **Skills transfer**. You want to provide coaching and mentoring to delivery teams in continuous integration (CI) and continuous delivery (CD) strategies. This may even include helping teams to setup their tooling, get them training in automated regression testing, and configuring their environments.

Security

The focus of the Security process blade is to describe how to protect your organization from both information/virtual and physical threats. This includes procedures for security governance, identity and access management, vulnerability management, security policy management, incident response, and vulnerability management. As you would expect these policies will affect your organization's strategies around change management, disaster recovery and business continuity, solution delivery, and vendor management. For security to be effective it has to be a fundamental aspect of your organizational culture.

Why is security important? Because security breaches can be devastating. For example, in January 2009 it was found that Heartland, a company that processed 100 million credit card transactions a month, had been breached via SQL injection in March 2008 [Heartland]. Found to be out of compliance with the PCI DSS security standards, they were not allowed to process the transactions of major credit card vendors until May 2009 and they had to pay out $145 million to cover fraudulent transactions. Or the November 2013 security breach at Target where the personal information of 70 million customers was compromised, the cost of the breach was $162 million, and the CEO resigned [Target].

The following strategies enable you to optimize your Security activities:

1. **Collaborate with the teams.** Security engineers will be invited to work with delivery teams to review their work for security concerns at the earliest feasible moment and in some cases to help them to secure critical aspects of their solutions.

2. **Support common security infrastructure.** Security engineers will help teams to identify and adopt appropriate security tooling and frameworks. They develop and evolve security guidance for your organization.

3. **Skills transfer.** Providing people with coaching and training in security will help to build security awareness within your organization. Security training should be provided to all members of your organization, with deeper training and education provided to IT staff who are directly involved with development or operations of secure systems.

4. **Collaborate with other organizations.** Within the security community there is constant sharing of information between organizations, including education about new security threats and new mitigation strategies.

Data Management

 Data management is "the development, execution and supervision of plans, policies, programs and practices that control, protect, deliver and enhance the value of data and information assets" [DAMA]. The Data Management process blade promotes a pragmatic, streamlined approach to data management that fits into the rest of your IT processes — we need to *Optimize Flow* across our overall activities, not locally sub-optimize our data management strategy. We need to support the overall needs of our organization while producing real value for our customers. Disciplined agile data management does this in an evolutionary and collaborative manner, via concrete data management strategies that provide the right data at the right time to the right people.

There are many reasons why data management is critical to your organization's success. Data is the lifeblood of your enterprise and needs to be treated like the corporate asset that it is. But it also needs to be available — people need to have appropriate access to (sufficiently) accurate data in a timely manner if your organization is to succeed in the marketplace. Furthermore, as discussed in Chapter 4, streamlined Data Management is an enabler of DevOps.

The internal workflow of a DA approach to data management is depicted in Figure 5.4[6]. Notice how data managers need to collaborate closely with others to evolve data artifacts such as meta data and enterprise data models, improve data quality (through techniques such as database refactoring), and evolve enterprise data guidance. Data management also includes the monitoring of operational data sources and the support and enablement of solution delivery teams.

To succeed your data management efforts need to be based on Disciplined Agile values such as:

1. **Evolution over definition**. Modern database development is evolutionary in nature as opposed to the big modeling up front (BMUF) strategies of traditional development. This requires adoption of pragmatic data quality techniques such as continuous database integration, database testing, and database refactoring [AgileData].

2. **Sufficiency over perfection**. All artifacts, including data-oriented ones, should be just barely good enough (JBGE), or sufficient, given the situation that you face. As a result you need to streamline and lean out your approaches to master data management, meta data management, and modeling in general. *Pragmatism* is critical for success.

3. **Collaboration over documentation**. Effective data managers work collaboratively with delivery teams, and others within your organization. As you can see in Figure 5.4 they actively transfer data knowledge and skills to others. Rapid feedback and decision making is critical for business agility. We commonly see data management groups as bottlenecks to the teams trying to deliver value on a frequent basis. Indeed this is often the reason that teams bypass data authorities altogether. Applying agile data strategies is key in your drive toward continuous delivery capability.

---

[6] Although we have diagrams like this posted on DisciplinedAgileDelivery.com for other process blades this is the only blade in this chapter for which we're showing the workflow. We do this for two reasons: To show how a modern approach to Data Management works in practice and to give you a feel for the wealth of information available to you about DA.

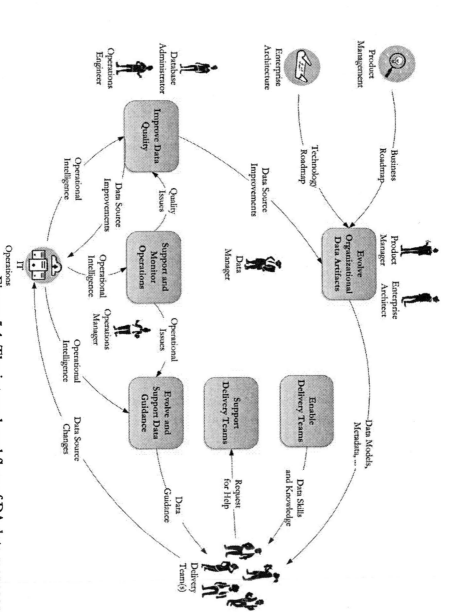

Figure 5.4. The internal workflow of DA data management.

97

4. **Automation over manual processes**. An important aspect of optimizing Data Management workflow is to automate database regression testing, database deployments, and verification against data standards to name just a few data-oriented activities.

Continuous Improvement

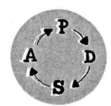

The purpose of the Continuous Improvement process blade is to enable people within your organization to easily share their improvement learnings with one another in a systematic way. This is important because it helps people to increase their skills and knowledge quicker, thereby speeding up your process improvement efforts. In effect it creates feedback loops between teams through which a learning culture emerges, increasing the chance that you're learning at both the team and organization levels. Your organization requires a mechanism for organizational learning that is at least as fast as the rate of change in the marketplace that you operate. By sharing the learnings from experiments you increase the return of investment (ROI) from running those experiments (when you share the learnings from a failed experiment agilists like to say that you maximize your "failure ROI").

There are several strategies that your organization can implement to support continuous improvement efforts at the organization level:

1. **Organize shared experiments**. What we're suggesting is that you experiment in an enterprise aware manner. When you have dozens or hundreds of teams working in parallel it makes a lot of sense to have several teams collaborate on experiments so that they can learn together. Your enterprise architecture team will include potential technical experiments in your organization's technical roadmap so they should coordinate shared experiments. Similarly Product Management will identify and then coordinate shared business experiments. By collaborating on experiments you increase your overall learning and open opportunities for more "radical" experimentation that would normally be beyond the scope of a single team.

2. **Organize learning events**. There are many ways that people can share learnings with one another, including "hackathons" where people from various teams collaborate to solve a problem, "lunch and learns" where someone presents their learnings, lean coffees where people interested in a given domain get together to discuss topics that interest them, internal learning events such as open

spaces or formal training, and cross-team retrospectives to name a few options.

3. **Support Communities of Practice (CoPs)/guilds.** A CoP is a group of people who share a craft or profession and who have voluntarily banded together to learn from each other to develop themselves and often even improve the organization. We've seen CoPs focused on agile software development, testing, architecture, management, coaching, business analysis, DevOps, and many more.

4. **Support Centers of Excellence/Expertise (CoEs).** A CoE is a group of people with specialized skills and expertise whose job is to provide leadership and purposely disseminate that knowledge within your organization. CoEs help other people and teams to *Be Awesome*. As you'll see in Chapter 7, you will likely want to establish a Disciplined Agile CoE to guide your agile transformation efforts.

Continuous improvement requires a mind shift for many people, and it certainly requires a culture shift for your organization. John Borthwick, the CEO of Betaworks, describes the required mindset well – "Each change, each innovation is considered to be the new normal, a new steady state when in fact the new normal is a state of continual innovation" [Borthwick]. Your organization is a complex adaptive system (CAS) that is constantly evolving as people experiment and learn, and this can be both exciting and frustrating at the same time. We explore Continuous Improvement in more detail in Chapter 8.

People Management

People management goes by many names, including human resource (HR) management, talent management, people operations, staff management, and work force management to name a few. The fundamental goal of the People Management process blade is to attract and retain great people who want to work on awesome teams. This is important because people and the way they work together are the primary determinant of your success. You also want to support people's career aspirations, helping them to become more fulfilled and to find the best way for them to add value. By offering greater employment flexibility your organization will be able to attract a more diverse range of people, thereby increasing your chances of attracting great people. Finally, many people-oriented activities fall outside the scope of what occurs on your work teams – many aspects of onboarding new staff and offboarding of existing staff for example, let alone working through the bigger picture of managing your organization's long-term staffing mix.

Critical activities of your People Management efforts include:

1. **Help people and teams to *Be Awesome*.** We really can't say this enough! To do this you will want to build and then support organizational mechanisms to help people find meaningful and purposeful work where they can excel.

2. **Address people problems.** Conflicts will occur between people. In many cases the people involved will resolve the issue themselves, but sometimes they will need outside help to quickly and fairly resolve the problem. This is one area where people managers, sometimes called resource managers, can help.

3. **Help your organization stay on the right side of the law.** Although the best people to determine whether someone will fit on a team is the existing team itself, there are still legal requirements regarding how you go about hiring someone. Similarly, in many countries there are legal requirements regarding how work is organized, how people are rewarded, how they are offboarded, and many other important concerns.

4. **Ensure long-term organizational sustainment.** Considering the "big picture", and taking long-term considerations into account becomes quite challenging in the People Management space. You need to address succession planning (how will you replace expertise when key people leave the company?), capacity planning (how many people do you need?), skills planning (what skills do you want to build within the company?), and communication around expectations and opportunities. All of these things require close collaboration and tight feedback loops with leadership, middle management, and front-line staff.

5. **Hire people who want to be agile.** Your criteria for who you hire must evolve to reflect the agile direction of your organization. Look for people with an agile mindset. Do they like to experiment and learn? Are they enterprise aware? Are they eager to collaborate with others? Also, look for people who would be a good fit on the team they are being hired into – agile is a team sport, and any new team member should enhance the team's ability to delight their customers. A recommended DA strategy is to let the team make the final decision regarding who is hired.

6. **Keep the right people.** You need to continually evolve your strategies to keep people engaged and committed to your organization year after year. This includes intervening when they

aren't happy or want the opportunity to try new things (including moving to another team).

7. **Set stretch goals for teams based on relative improvement.** In *Beyond Budgeting* Hope and Fraser recommend that you set goals for teams based on maximizing their short and long-term performance potential. Better yet teams should set their own goals, with leadership asking them "What can you do if you really try?" and "What's the best possible outcome if everything goes right?" to get them to motivate themselves. These aspirational goals are often disconnected from performance evaluation and rewards so that

Not Everyone Wants to Become Agile
A significant challenge faced by many organizations when they begin moving towards a more agile approach is they realize that some people are "agile unfriendly." For example, asking people to become generalizing specialists is difficult when they've built their careers on being a specialist. The marketplace still looks for people who are specialized, because many HR departments have yet to embrace agile and because your existing processes are based on people being specialized. It's uncomfortable for some business people to be asked to be part of delivery teams, and it can be equally uncomfortable to ask developers to interact directly with their stakeholders. The point is that some people will choose not to make the agile journey with you, and that's ok as there are likely other traditional projects for which they could productively contribute.

they remain motivational. For performance measures, a better strategy is to measure how the team has improved over time and if possible to compare them to their industry competitors. We have also seen many companies moving away from annual performance reviews and management by objectives (MBO). These approaches are now being seen as: having feedback that is too infrequent, thus discouraging necessary change; and generally inconsistent with adaptive and collaborative work.

8. **Build systems for happiness.** In *Management 3.0* Jurgen Appelo describes the challenges of managing organizations and teams given that they are complex adaptive systems (CAS), growing, changing, and learning all the time. He describes modern management approaches to create the right conditions to foster

high performance teams. Similarly, in *Joy Inc.*, Richard Sheridan describes how his company Menlo Innovations has grown a corporate culture that creates true joy for those that work for his company as well as his customers.

9. **Understand the IT domain**. People management for IT is hard, in part because of the nature of IT people and mostly because of how rapidly IT evolves. Regardless, you need to get on top of this to be effective, and many organizations struggle to do so. For example, it's quite common to see IT job ads asking for 5 years of experience in a technology that has existed for 2 years or ads asking for a laundry list of expertise that would require several lifetimes to gain. What do you think ads like that say about your company, particularly to potential candidates whom you'd love to hire?

(Lean) IT Governance

 IT Governance encompasses the leadership, organizational structures and streamlined processes to enable IT to work as a partner in sustaining and extending the organization's ability to produce meaningful value for its customers. IT governance is part of your organization's overall corporate governance (Control) strategy. IT governance encompasses several more narrow forms of governance, including but not limited to the governance of IT delivery/development, data/information, IT security, IT investment, enterprise architecture, and IT operations activities. Although many agilists don't like the idea of governance, the fact is that you're being governed, like it or not. We believe that you deserve to be governed effectively which is why we've built governance into all levels of the DA framework, an aspect of *Enterprise Awareness*. DA takes a comprehensive approach to strategy so that it is coherent, consistent, and effective across your organization – when governance strategies are implemented disparately (there's a security governance strategy, a data governance strategy, a financial governance strategy, …) you inevitably cause havoc across your teams because the governance strategies contradict each other in places while at other times gaping holes exist because everyone thought someone else was covering that area. And, due to the danger of governance efforts doing more harm than good, we're firm believers in keeping governance as lean and lightweight as possible.

There are several reasons why you want to embrace IT governance. You want to ensure that:

- Your organization's IT investment is spent wisely
- Your IT strategy supports your organization's needs
- Your IT teams are empowered to carry out their work
- People are motivated to work together effectively
- Risks are monitored and mitigated at appropriate places in your organization
- Your IT infrastructure is sound
- Everyone within IT works in an open and collaborative manner
- All work is completely transparent to all stakeholders
- Lines of accountability are clear
- All of these things will continue to be true now and into the future (you don't want short-term decisions to harm you in the long term)

To successfully take a lean approach to IT governance you should adopt the following strategies:

1. **Lead by example**. People mirror the behaviors of senior management. If you want your staff to be open, collaborative, enterprise aware, willing to learn through experimentation, to be trustworthy, to be respectful of others, and to focus on delighting your customers then you must visibly and consistently be doing these things yourself. When Bill Gates was CEO of Microsoft he would fly economy class, just like every other Microsoft employee, to reinforce Microsoft's value of spending their money wisely. Contrast this with Ginni Rometty, CEO of IBM, who in May 2017 flew to the IBM Hursley labs in a helicopter at a time when any travel over £75 required senior executive approval [IBM] – what values do you think she was reinforcing with that leadership behavior?

2. **Prefer motivation over command and control**. Effective governance strategies motivate people to do what is right (however "right" is defined for your organization). People are motivated by a sense of mastery, by having autonomy to do their work, and through purpose [Pink]. When you motivate people they are much more likely to do what you want than if you simply tell them to do it.

3. **Prefer enablement over audit**. It is human nature to take the easy path. What this tells us is if you focus on making the things you want to happen easy (you enable them), and the things that you don't want to happen difficult, then chances are very good that people will do what you want. In combination with motivation, this allows you to take a "trust but verify" strategy

where lightweight monitoring, instead of heavyweight auditing, is sufficient for most situations. It also enables you to move away from reviewing documents, which you can never guarantee are used for anything more than passing a review, and instead focus on mitigating risk. Pixar CEO Ed Catmull describes this mindset well in his book *Creativity, Inc.* – "Management must loosen the controls, not tighten them. They must accept risk; they must trust the people they work with and strive to clear the path for them; They must pay attention to and engage with anything that creates fear" [CreativityInc].

4. **Communicate continuously**. The only way people will know what your organization expects of them is when it is clearly and regularly communicated to them. What are your organizational goals (purpose)? Why are they important (mastery)? How will you help people to fulfill these goals (autonomy)?

5. **Streamline collaboration**. A significant part of leadership is to make it as easy as possible for people to work together, and in particular to help *Optimize Workflow* and information sharing between teams.

6. **Be transparent**. Transparency is a fundamental concept for agile teams – they should make all work in progress clearly visible and their status easily consumable by their stakeholders. Transparency is a two-way street in that management should make their thinking, strategies, and organizational results available to their staff as well. This promotes greater trust and supports *Enterprise Awareness*.

7. **Enable continuous improvement**. People, and teams in general, should strive to continuously learn and improve. Your governance strategy should promote this through recognizing that teams will organize themselves and their work processes to reflect their situation (*Context Counts*). It should also allow teams to run experiments to discover what works for them (and what doesn't).

8. **Consider both the long and short term**. An important goal of your governance activities is to ensure that you operate effectively today while positioning yourself for long-term success – you do not want to make the mistake of putting your long-term viability at risk in the pursuit of short-term profits.

9. **Take a holistic approach**. Effective IT governance addresses all of IT. Some organizations make the mistake of having their Portfolio Mangers be responsible for governance, but when that happens the technical aspects of governance tend to be missed in

favor of financial governance. Another important observation is that you cannot limit your strategy to just agile governance – traditional teams will still need to be governed in a traditional manner.

In addition to the above strategies there are also strategies from the Control process blade (Chapter 6) that may be applicable for IT Governance. These strategies are: Ensure personal safety and experimentation; Promote self-organizing teams; Prefer guidelines over edicts; Create sandboxes; Mission command over rigid instructions; Collect actionable metrics; Prefer real-time automated dashboards; Measure customer outcomes; Manage for throughput over utilization; Transparency for everyone enables control; Provide audit guidance to teams; and Govern by exception.

Enterprise Architecture

An agile enterprise architecture is a flexible, easily extended, and easily evolved collection of structures and processes upon which your organization is built. The activity of agile enterprise architecture is the collaborative and evolutionary exploration and modeling of an organization's architectural ecosystem in a context-sensitive manner. The implications are that enterprise architects must be willing to work in a collaborative and flexible manner and solution delivery teams must be willing to work closely with enterprise architects.

Why should you invest in enterprise architecture? Having a common architecture vision to work towards enables agile teams to focus on value creation. Having common architectural guidance enables greater consistency, which increases quality and that in turn enables teams to react quicker to marketplace changes. Agile architectures enable disaggregation of your IT assets which in turn increases the opportunities for reuse, leading once again to greater quality and greater ability to deliver quickly. A common infrastructure enables continuous delivery practices which are an important part of your Disciplined DevOps strategy (see Chapter 4). Finally, enterprise architecture scales agile delivery by enabling teams to work together on more complex solutions.

There are several strategies that we see applied in effective enterprise architecture efforts:

1. **Collaborative architecture.** Your enterprise architects (EAs) should work closely with the delivery teams to guide them in your organization's EA strategy. This will help to increase

their productivity, increase the quality of their work, and reduce the chance that the team introduces new technical debt into your ecosystem. Particularly in smaller organizations an EA will take on the role of Architecture Owner (AO) on one or more delivery teams.

2. **Rolling-wave roadmapping.** Figure 5.5 shows an example of a rolling wave technology roadmap as of September 2016 for a medium sized organization. In the near term concrete and specific activities are called out whereas the farther out in time something is the vaguer it is. Also notice how there are several swimlanes – planned upgrades, experiments, reusable infrastructure, and retirements (stuff to be removed from production) – are called out. On a regular basis this roadmap is updated by the EAs based on the needs of, and current vision for, your organization.

3. **Skills transfer.** The EAs should actively transfer their architecture skills and thinking to others within your organization, in particular to the AOs within the delivery teams. This will help them to learn skills to *Be Awesome*.

4. **Agile architecture guidelines**. The EAs are typically responsible for leading the development and evolution of architecture guidelines, collaborating with the delivery teams to do so.

Figure 5.5. Rolling wave technology roadmap.

	Sept-Oct 2016	Nov 2016 - Feb 2017	March 2017 – August 2017	Sept 2017+
Planned Upgrades	- Logging Microservice Oct 14 - Messaging Microservice Oct 28	- MySQL 5.7 Dec 3	- Windows 10.1 - Security Microservice	- MySQL Cloud
Experiments	- MongoDB - Zurb Foundation	- Cassandra - Couchbase - Windows 10.1	- MySQL Cloud	- TBD
Reusable Infrastructure	- Security Microservice Sept 30	- Email Microservice Nov 15	- Persistence Microservice - Transaction Microservice	- TBD
Retire	- SQLServer	- SQLServer Feb 5 - DB2	- DB2 - Greenbow	- CICS - COBOL

Reuse Engineering

The Reuse Engineering process blade addresses the purposeful rescue, creation, management, support, and governance of reusable assets. Reuse engineering is often guided by your organization's enterprise architecture team, although Disciplined Agile IT organizations tend to fund a specific reuse engineering team. There are several reasons why you want to implement the Reuse Engineering process blade, including: quicker time to market (you have less to build); improved ROI (you have less to pay for); improved functional consistency (you reuse common assets); easier updates to common functionality (you have

Reuse Engineering is Really Hard!
Reuse Engineering usually proves to be the most difficult of all the process blades for an organization to implement. Reuse is very easy to talk about, but very difficult to be successful at in practice because of the skill required and the swiftly changing nature of the underlying technologies and business needs. Reuse relies on true *Enterprise Awareness* within delivery teams, something that comes with experience and time rather than management decree.

less things to update); improved development consistency (reusable assets provide examples of how things should be designed and built); improved quality (you're more likely to expose hidden defects in assets that are widely used); and reduced technical debt (due to greater quality and fewer assets).

When you choose to implement Reuse Engineering, you will typically want to consider the following strategies:

1. **Have a reuse engineering team**. Because it is easy for reuse to fall to the wayside in favor of short-term actions, it is often best to invest in a specific team of reuse engineers. This team will monitor what is happening on the delivery teams, often being involved in the enterprise architecture coordination sessions with the Architecture Owners on the delivery teams. The reuse team will harvest potentially reusable assets, clean them up, reintegrate the assets back into the work of the source team, coach teams in reusing existing assets, and help the teams to reuse appropriate assets.

2. **Architect for reuse**. Your Reuse Engineers will work with the Enterprise Architects to identify potentially reusable assets that can be either developed or purchased when it makes the

most sense for the delivery teams that need them. This will require you to work through how this asset fits into the overall enterprise architecture, where it fits on your technology roadmap (see Figure 5.5), and in the case of assets that you're building to identify it's interface via an API-first strategy [APIFirst].

3. **Keep the feedback cycle short**. Enterprise staff have in the past been bottlenecks for agile teams due to slow turnaround of services contracts/APIs and data schema changes. You need to balance enterprise interests with the needs for rapid decision making for the teams. DA recommends a practice called look-ahead modeling to look ahead at upcoming work where architecting for reuse is required to give your reuse engineers the necessary time to come up with the appropriate solution for the teams.

4. **Fund reuse directly**. Your reuse engineering team, if you have one, should have its own budget. The quickest way you can kill a reuse program is to charge delivery teams for any help they receive from the reuse team or for reusing any assets. When you charge teams for these things you are in effect punishing them for reuse.

5. **Measure the value of reuse**. The benefits of reuse are increased quality, quicker time to market, and lower development costs (to name a few). Because these benefits are affected by a myriad of other factors, in can be hard to tease out the benefits derived solely from greater reuse.

6. **Quality over quantity**. It is better to have a small number of high-quality reusable assets than a large number of questionable assets that people aren't interested in. Something is reusable only when it's been successfully reused several times, not just because you declare it to be reusable.

Portfolio Management

 The Portfolio Management process blade addresses how an IT organization goes about identifying, prioritizing, organizing, and governing their various IT endeavors. Disciplined Agile Portfolio Management seeks to do this in a lightweight and streamlined manner that maximizes the creation of business value in a long-term sustainable manner. IT endeavors typically include solution delivery initiatives/projects, stable product development teams, business

experiments (along the lines of a lean startup strategy), and the operation of existing IT-based solutions. Portfolio Management is critical to your IT success in that it determines where IT investment will be made, it coordinates your IT efforts, and it ensures ongoing IT investment is wisely spent.

Disciplined Agile approaches to Portfolio Management will address the following issues:

1. **Spend IT investment wisely.** You need to decide which efforts (projects, product teams, experiments, …) to fund. Agile Portfolio Managers focus on value delivery over cost and will strive to reduce the cost of delay throughout their portfolio. The concept of the cost of delay is straightforward – if a feature is going to provide value to a customer then you will reap the most value from it by getting it into their hands quickly. From a management point of view, this is a key aspect of opportunity cost. They work closely with Finance (Chapter 6) to achieve this.

2. **Balance exploring new business with exploiting existing value streams.** The Three Horizon Model, see Figure 5.6, provides insight into how your IT budget will be allocated: the majority of it will go to operating and evolving your current solutions, some will go towards new development in support of creating new value streams, and some will go to exploratory efforts to identify potential future value streams [McKinsey].

3. **Monitor and guide ongoing initiatives.** To ensure that your organization is getting good value for their IT investment you must monitor the ongoing initiatives in both development and operations. Yes, you want to respect and trust your people but you also need to verify how things are working out and guide them to better outcomes where needed. The goal is to ensure that the ongoing efforts are aligned with one another.

4. **Rolling-wave budgeting and planning.** Once again, a rolling wave approach to budgeting and planning proves more effective than traditional annual approaches. This is an important aspect of a "beyond budgeting" approach [HopeFraser].

5. **Prefer small initiatives over large initiatives.** Small initiatives tend to be lower risk than larger ones, provide greater flexibility in how you stream work to your teams, and lower your cost of delay by enabling you to release functionality quicker into production [Reinertsen].

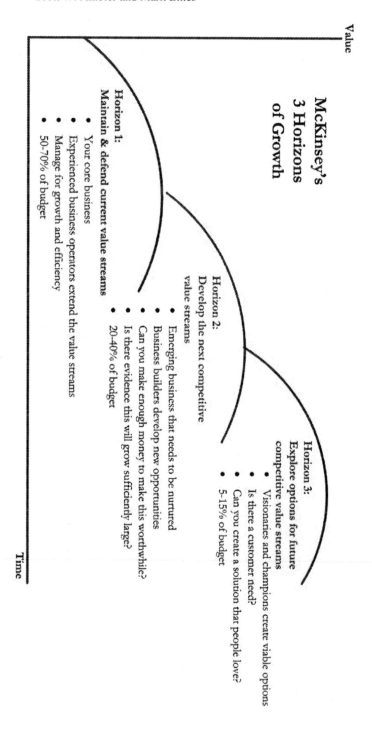

McKinsey's 3 Horizons of Growth

Horizon 1:
Maintain & defend current value streams

- Your core business
- Experienced business operators extend the value streams
- Manage for growth and efficiency
- 50-70% of budget

Horizon 2:
Develop the next competitive value streams

- Emerging business that needs to be nurtured
- Business builders develop new opportunities
- Can you make enough money to make this worthwhile?
- Is there evidence this will grow sufficiently large?
- 20-40% of budget

Horizon 3:
Explore options for future competitive value streams

- Visionaries and champions create viable options
- Is there a customer need?
- Can you create a solution that people love?
- 5-15% of budget

Value

Time

Figure 5.6. The McKinsey 3 Horizon model of growth.

6. **Cull "failures" quickly**. When you take an experimentation mindset with your portfolio management efforts, a key aspect of business agility, not everything you do will succeed. This is perfectly OK as long as you choose to learn from the experience and you cull the "failures" as quickly as possible. Figure 5.7 depicts the profitability of your portfolio, showing several types of initiatives. These initiatives are sorted in order of profitability on the diagram, in practice they would be running in parallel, potentially being worked on by teams that are side-by-side. First are "failed" marketplace experiments, ideas that you decided to invest in to (dis)prove via the Lean Startup-based exploratory lifecycle. These "failed experiments" are actually successes because you quickly and inexpensively discovered what the marketplace doesn't want. Second are failed solution development efforts. These were successful experiments but for some reason you decided to cancel them midway through development, often the result of a milestone decision that determined the product wasn't technically feasible or financially feasible any more. Third are value streams that were taken to market but unfortunately failed, either losing money or not making enough money to justify continuing forward with. Last are the value streams that are market successes from which you make the majority of your revenue (the Horizon 1 value streams).

7. **Invest in quality**. It's not just about funding new functionality. Your organization very likely has a serious technical debt problem that it needs to pay down. Regardless of how you do so – via small refactorings, via small technical stories, via explicit projects, via system replacements – this work must be explicitly funded [TechDebt]. At one of our customers, a large American Insurance company, fifty percent of their new development budget has been allocated for the next three to five years for paying down technical debt. Although this is painful in the short term, they are making this investment now so as to become more competitive in the long term. Having said all this, the cheapest technical debt to pay down is that which you don't incur in the first place. Architecture activities are built into the DA framework at both the delivery team and organizational levels to help teams avoid injecting new technical debt into your organizational ecosystem.

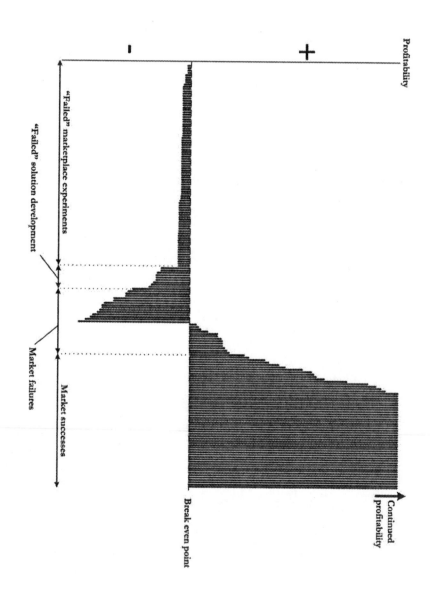

Figure 5.7. The profitability of your portfolio.

8. **Enable team effectiveness**. Your approach to Portfolio Management can have a significant impact on the effectiveness of your delivery teams. For example, choosing to fund stable, dedicated, long-lived delivery teams instead of short-term project teams provides teams with the opportunity and motivation to optimize the way that they work (remember the principle *Optimize Flow*). Aligning these teams to value streams, and adjusting over time, also enables greater effectiveness.

Product Management

 The Product Management process blade includes the activities around identifying and evolving your organization's business vision; of identifying and prioritizing potential products/solutions to support that vision; of identifying, prioritizing, and allocating features to products under development; of managing functional dependencies between products; and of marketing those products to their potential customers. Disciplined agile product management is product management performed in a collaborative and evolutionary manner that reflects the context of your organization.

There are several reasons why you want to adopt a DA approach to Product Management. Fundamentally you want to ensure that you're building the right products and by implication you're not still expending effort on the wrong products (or at least you stop doing so). You also want to ensure that you're bringing products and services to market at the right time, and that your offerings have the features that people want. Finally, effective product management will help to ensure that people are delighted to buy/use your offerings.

The critical activities of Product Management include:

1. **Rolling-wave planning**. With rolling wave planning you plan the work that you're about to do in detail, and any work that is in the future is planned at a higher level; the further out in time something is the vaguer your ideas for it are. This enables you to plan in advance, plan in detail the work you are just about to do and defer commitment on future issues that are likely to change anyway.

2. **Development of roadmaps**. Figure 5.8 depicts a rolling wave product roadmap – notice how functionality that is about to be implemented is described using granular user stories (a pragmatic feature-based approach), yet functionality that is several months away from being addressed is captured in the

113

form of capabilities/themes that are outcome-based. Such roadmaps help to set expectations for end users, or potential end users, of those products as well as guide the efforts of the delivery teams working on them. By taking an outcomes-based approach for the long-term you avoid locking in on functionality that might not work or might not be needed too early. Figure 5.9 depicts a rolling wave business roadmap (sometimes called a "products roadmap") that indicates forthcoming product releases. This is critical to help set customer expectations and for capacity planning (from the looks of it PurpleBow and MagicWand will start up once people are available from wrapping up development on Greenbow).

3. **Working closely with customers.** People in the Product Management role will work closely with existing customers as well as potential customers to understand what their needs are. The goal is to get a sense of what the marketplace wants so that your organization can respond effectively with the right products and services.

Figure 5.8. Rolling wave product roadmap for a single product.

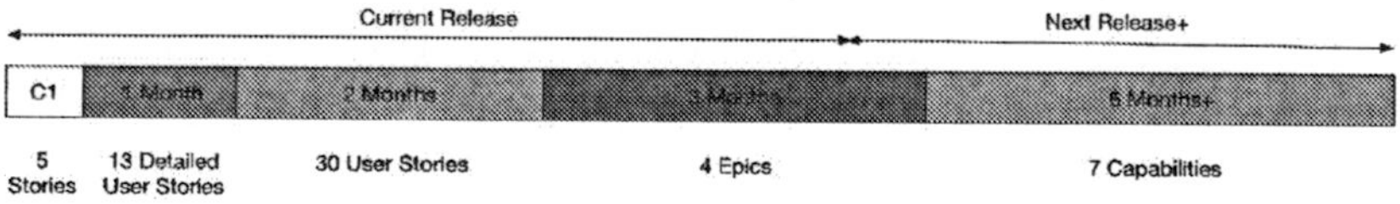

Figure 5.9. Rolling wave business/product(s) roadmap for an organization.

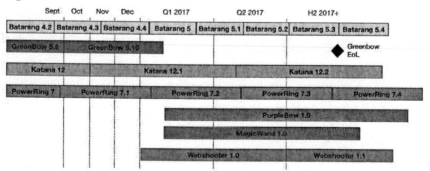

4. **Supporting delivery teams**. From the point of view of a Product Manager a Product Owner (PO) is someone that they must work closely with to get the solution that they envision. From the point of view of a PO the Product Manager is a key stakeholder for the product who provides strategic vision as well overall priorities. As seen in Figure 5.8, POs tend to focus on the story and epic level whereas Product Managers are focused on epics and capabilities/themes – the conversion of capabilities to epics, as well as prioritization of what needs to be accomplished in the short term, is where POs and Product Managers will collaborate regularly.

5. **Merging top-down and bottom-up planning**. Product Managers focus on long-term, strategic issues whereas POs tend to focus on tactical day-to-day concerns. The long-term capabilities and themes that the Product Managers focus on is top-down planning, as is breaking capabilities down into epics and stories. Bottom-up planning occurs when Product Owners bring new, often granular ideas to the conversation to determine where on the roadmap, if at all, they fit. You will achieve better balance by merging the top-down strategic concerns with bottom-up tactical concerns.

Disciplined Agile IT Enables Disciplined Agile Enterprises

This chapter provided a brief overview of the process blades of Disciplined Agile IT (DAIT). Greater detail, such as goal diagrams, workflow diagrams, and sometimes work product examples, can be found at DisciplinedAgileDelivery.com. Our focus was on process, not on organizational structure – every organization is different. Part of your overall agile transformation effort (Chapter 7) and continuous improvement effort (Chapter 8) is to guide your teams through identifying who will take on what activities.

Your Disciplined Agile IT department is an important part, and a key enabler of, your Disciplined Agile Enterprise (DAE). In the next chapter we will see how it all fits together and enables business agility.

6 THE DISCIPLINED AGILE ENTERPRISE

In previous chapters we focused on IT, starting with Disciplined Agile Delivery (DAD) in Chapter 3, Disciplined DevOps in Chapter 4, and Disciplined Agile IT (DAIT) in Chapter 5. This was important because software, and IT in general, is the key enabler of business agility. But it isn't enough, you also need an organization that can leverage your IT capabilities in the marketplace. The other business processes within your organization, see Figure 6.1 below, must also work in an adaptive and continuous manner.

This chapter describes how a Disciplined Agile Enterprise (DAE) looks like in practice. Let's start with several ideas that are foundational for a DAE:

1. **Your organization and your people must be agile**. Although our focus in this book is on effective process, the reality is that your organizational culture is the most important factor in your business agility success. You need people who strive to *Be Awesome* by collaborating in an *Enterprise Aware* manner to *Delight Customers* and continuously improve. Having said that, there is unfortunately little advice out there as to how an agile organization works as a whole, which is why in this book we choose to address that very topic. Coherence of your overall approach is critical – if one group of people is going in a different direction, if they aren't working in an agile manner, they will drag down your entire organization.

2. **It's all about value streams**. Your organization implements one or more value streams to provide value to your customers. A value stream is in effect a thread through your organization (and potentially partner organizations) of people collaborating to earn revenue. The best value streams *Delight Customers*, and part of doing that is to *Optimize the Flow* of your work to be reactive to customer needs.

3. **There is no one right answer**. Not only is every organization different, it is also evolving over time; Because *Context Counts* you must identify an approach that works for you. Prescriptive methods are attractive because they appear to be something you can quickly learn and install. However, the reality is that you need to choose the strategies that reflect your actual situation to be effective – *Choice is Good*. And of course *Pragmatism* should drive your choices, not a desire to "be agile."

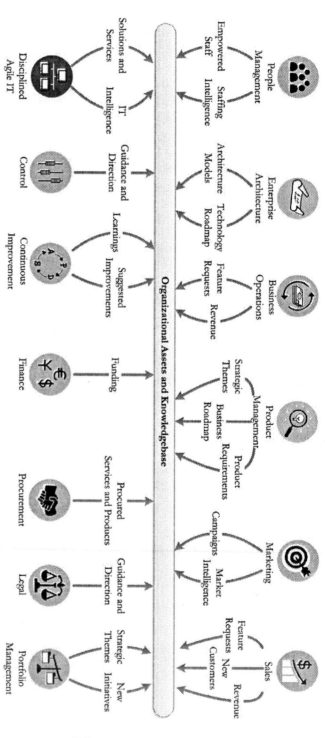

Figure 6.1. The process blades of a Disciplined Agile Enterprise.

4. **You need to sense and respond**. Gone are the days of annual planning and three to five year roadmaps. DAEs follow an adaptive, outcome-driven approach based on experimentation and probing/sensing their environment and then responding.
5. **You must be a learning organization**. Everyone is responsible for learning and sharing their skills, regardless of the organizational domain that they're working in. Because the modern marketplace evolves swiftly in unpredictable ways, you must be willing to experiment and to continually change your strategy to *Optimize Flow*. Furthermore, knowledge and knowledge work is becoming increasingly more important in modern enterprises, illuminating the need for continual learning.
6. **Self-organizing teams need fast access to resources**. Provide teams with the authority and responsibility to delight their customers. Senior leadership must help teams get the people, funding, help, and other resources that they require to react quickly to a marketplace opportunity; provide boundaries within which to operate; and provide an internal market for operational resources. Your objective is to match resource needs to prevailing customer demand – The implication is that some people may not be fully utilized, but this slack enables strategic work such as learning and improvement.

Teal is the New Black

Just as your process must be flexible and adaptive, so must your organization. In *Reinventing Organizations* Frederick Laloux works through the history of, and arguably a maturity model for, organizational design [Laloux]. The premise, which is overviewed in Figure 6.2, is that over time we're seeing organizations evolve from tribal and often violent structures (Red) through more formalized hierarchical structures (Amber/Orange) to agile approaches (Green) and finally DA approaches (Teal). Today the vast majority of organizations, believed to be 80-90%, are somewhere on the Amber through Green scale.

Figure 6.2. What color is your organization?

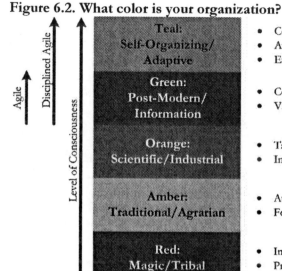

- Teal: Self-Organizing/Adaptive
  - Cellular, living organism
  - Awareness, fullfillment
  - Evolutionary purpose
- Green: Post-Modern/Information
  - Consensus/participative style
  - Values-based motivational culture
- Orange: Scientific/Industrial
  - Task oriented, profit/growth focus
  - Innovative/meritocracy management style
- Amber: Traditional/Agrarian
  - Authoritarian, security protocol modality
  - Formal roles and hierarchy
- Red: Magic/Tribal
  - Impulsive, survival urgency modality
  - Predator/prey management style

Adapted from *Reinventing Organizations* by Frederic Laloux

There are several important observations we'd like to make about Laloux's organizational maturity scale:

1. **Green and teal align well with agile**. For your organization to support Disciplined Agile it should at least be (mostly) Green, with a participative and values-based culture, or better yet Teal with a truly adaptive and aware strategy (as we've promoted throughout this chapter).

2. **Start where you are**. Your organization will start its improvement journey wherever it currently is on the scale. Laloux's model provides insights into what your current challenges are likely to be and what potential improvements you should consider making.

3. **You can still benefit from becoming more agile or lean**. Teams can still be agile within Orange and Amber organizations, but the organization itself will struggle with agility due to cultural impediments. It is difficult to jump organizational levels – in other words if your organization is currently Amber then you need to move through Orange, then Green, and finally Teal.

4. **It's really hard to move between levels**. Laloux says that the only way to become Teal, and by implication to evolve to any level, is to have the express support of the company founder/CEO and the owners of the company. This is similar to our experience, and in Chapter 7 when we describe how to go

about an agile transformation we also add that you need the explicit support of the front-line workers too. Laloux himself recommends that you focus on becoming the best Amber, or best Orange, organization that you can be so as to not have to fight the cultural inertia within your organization. In other words, focus on continuous improvement (the subject of chapter 8) rather than transformation.

Why does your organization need to be at least Green or Teal to become truly agile? Green organizations support a participative culture style that enables collaboration within and between teams. Green organizations explicitly align people around common values, so injecting any missing agile and lean philosophies often proves to be straightforward. This is clearly needed for an agile culture to thrive. Teal organizations go one step further and bring it all together by explicitly recognizing that they are complex adaptive systems (CASs). This provides an environment where agile

> **Your Organization is Probably a Rainbow**
> It's attractive to think that your organizational culture is consistent across the entire enterprise, but it is far more likely that you have teams or divisions with differing color ratings according to Laloux's model. This is because the culture of a team (or division) is greatly influenced by the leader of that team, and leaders vary in their style. Because teams face unique situations — sometimes a red strategy is the most appropriate given what the team faces. *Context counts!*

teams are able to experiment, learn, collaborate, and most importantly thrive as they find new ways to delight their customers. Teal organizations are much closer to communities than they are to traditional corporate structures.

From Lines of Business to Value Streams

A value stream is the process(es) of creating, producing, and delivering a good or service to the market. A value stream may be internal to a company, or it may include external suppliers in addition to the internal processes required to leverage them. A value stream starts and ends with the customer in mind. What problems or needs do they have? What can we do to fulfill them? How can we delight the customer in how we do so? How can we do better? All critical questions you should continuously ask as an organization.

Value streams are threads through your organization and your process. Value streams encompass all the people, resources, and activities required to provide one or more offerings to customers. In Figure 6.3 you see that there are two value streams, two threads, through your organization's processes. Large organizations may have dozens if not hundreds of value streams and any given customer may be involved with several value streams. For example, a financial institution will have value streams around retail banking services, home mortgages, premiere mortgage management, corporate mortgage management, construction loan management, online brokerage, private brokerage, and many more.

Figure 6.3. Value streams thread through your process.

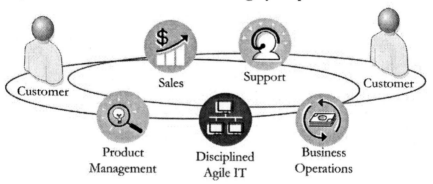

From a DA point of view a value stream will encompass activities such as solution delivery, operations and support of that solution, product management for the products that support the value stream, governance within the value stream, security, and so on. In short, there are many process blades that support the value streams that are not shown in Figure 6.3 (for the sake of simplicity). Yet at the same time there are aspects of process blades such as Finance, People Management, or Enterprise Architecture that go beyond value streams.

Isn't a value stream just a fancy new term for a line of business (LoB)? Not exactly. A LoB is a corporate group or division that is focused on providing a product or set of related projects to serve a particular customer need. The primary difference is that a LoB typically involves the creation of a group, with all the organizational baggage that entails – LoBs tend to become political empires within an enterprise that often evolves into something that exists for the sole purpose of existing. A value stream, on the other hand, brings together the people and resources required to serve the customer with the knowledge that the value stream will adapt to meet the evolving needs of the customer. Many value streams prove to be short-lived, with lifespans ranging from a few months to decades. Value streams require greater organizational agility and discipline than what is commonly exhibited by traditional LoBs.

Disciplined Agile IT

Chapter 5 overviewed how Disciplined Agile IT (DAIT) develops, operates, and evolves IT-based solutions to support your organization's value streams. For your organization to successfully evolve into a DAE it is critical that business leaders understand the realities of IT and are able to leverage it appropriately. To do so, business leaders must adopt a Disciplined Agile mindset regarding IT:

1. **IT cannot be treated like a "black box."** Black box is a technical term that refers to something that you provide inputs to, outputs are produced, but you don't know the internal workings of how it is accomplished. Gone are the days when you could provide your requirements to IT, wait for several months (or years), be involved with some last minute testing, and then lament that the provided solution didn't really meet your needs. As an executive you must learn how IT works in practice, you must understand how your financing and control/governance impact IT's ability to function, and most importantly discover that the only way to get solutions that meet your real needs is to actively work with your IT colleagues.

2. **IT is your primary competitive advantage.** Because modern organizations are being more and more dependent on knowledge work, IT may be the only sustainable advantage that you have over the long term, and then only if you continually learn and improve. You're trying to compete on price? That's a race to the bottom and in most cases requires better IT to squeeze out costs. You're trying to compete on flexibility of options? That definitely requires sophisticated IT if you hope to scale. For example, the incredible variety of Lego™ products (there are 53 different colors, over 2300 types of elements/bricks, and 19 billion elements are produced annually) is the direct result of sophisticated automation [Lego].

3. **IT deserves a seat at the management table.** In many organizations, particularly those in the technology industry, IT is now at the head of the table.

4. **IT must work collaboratively with the rest of the organization.** IT is only one of many important aspects of your organization, which the rest of this chapter makes clear.

Marketing

 The raison d'être for Marketing, sometimes called brand management, is to ensure successful interactions between your organization and the outside world. Your Marketing efforts will represent your organization and your offerings, both products and services, to the outside world and conversely will represent customers, and potential customers, to the rest of the organization. In conjunction with Product Management (see Chapter 5), Marketing will be actively involved with long-term visioning for your organization's offerings.

A good definition of Agile Marketing comes from McKinsey – "[Agile marketing] means using data and analytics to continuously source promising opportunities or solutions to problems in real time, deploying tests quickly, evaluating the results, and rapidly iterating. At scale, a high-functioning agile marketing organization can run hundreds of campaigns simultaneously and multiple new ideas every week" [McKinseyMarketing]. The Agile Marketing Manifesto, first developed in 2012, also provides significant insights about how to apply an agile approach to your marketing efforts [MarketingManifesto]. This includes taking a validated learning approach, being customer focused, working in a collaborative and flexible manner, and working in an evolutionary (iterative and incremental) manner.

Our experience from working with numerous organizations worldwide is that Marketing by its very nature tends to be agile and that most organizations find they just need to make a few improvements to their current approach. These changes potentially include:

1. **Sell the sizzle, not the steak.** This is an old marketing adage that is particularly pertinent for DAEs. You want to move away from marketing products and features, both of which may have very short lifecycles in today's marketplace, and towards campaigns built on brand and the benefits provided by your offerings. For example, many car advertisements on television focus on how you can get out into the wilderness and enjoy life, or go to the beach to surf, or go out with your friends. They may tell you a few key facts such as gas mileage or horsepower, but they never go into details about the gearing of the transmission, the size of the gas tank, or the cleaning capability of the windshield wipers.

2. **Prefer marketplace experiments over focus groups.** Taking a validated learning approach with test campaigns and then quantifying the impact has been common practice within marketing for years. Your goal is to use sophisticated

experiments to measure the overall impact of your marketing strategies and then apply these insights to improving both your offerings and the marketing of those offerings.

3. **Market marketing**. Many marketing teams find that they need to market themselves to the rest of the organization, particularly to the IT delivery teams to whom marketers are a key stakeholder. Your marketing efforts must be fully integrated into the value stream teams that they support.

4. **Customer discovery over static prediction**. This is one of the values of the Agile Marketing Manifesto, promoting the observation that you must observe and interact with your (potential) customers to determine what they want. The Cynefin framework teaches us that complex problems where the solution is not predictable up front, problems typically faced by Marketing teams, are best solved with a probe and respond strategy such as this [Cynefin]. Traditional marketing strategies involve far too much detailed guessing or prediction of what people want, increasing both the cost of delay and the risk of missing the mark entirely.

5. **Gain insights through targeted analytics**. In addition to the insights provided by validated learning you also want to leverage the wealth of information provided by analytics. You want to integrate data generated in-house with acquired data from external sources (often the result of "big data" analytics). The aim of these insights should be to identify anomalies, pain points, issues, or customer opportunities. Better yet, use predictive analytics to identify the potentially most profitable customers through analysis of the lifecycle of customer purchases and behavior [DavenportHarris]. It's important to note that your existing marketing campaigns, such as your loyalty program, can be important sources of data. Similarly, marketing via social media platforms such as Facebook and LinkedIn will also produce a wealth of information about customer behaviors.

6. **Provide stakeholders to IT delivery teams**. Your marketing team can be a critical source of stakeholders for IT teams, including themselves, actual customers, and perhaps even potential customers. As we learned in Chapter 3, active stakeholder participation is vital to the success of IT solution delivery.

Sales

 The aim of your Sales effort is to, you guessed it, sell your organization's offerings (both products and services) to customers. Your sales people, if any, will work very closely with your Marketing team to ensure they are focused on selling offerings that reflect your organizations' overall strategy. They will also work closely with IT to ensure that what they're selling is available or can be built in a timely manner. Organizationally Sales is often combined with Marketing or may even be matrixed into Business Operations.

Even when your direct sales processes are fully automated, such as with online sales at sites such as Amazon, eBay, Etsy, or many more, you still need to understand and optimize your sales processes over time. For example, e-commerce firms are constantly experimenting with new ways to sell their wares, occasionally even identifying patentable techniques. They are actively analyzing sales data, looking for patterns in customer behavior and new opportunities. The goal is to learn, often in real time, what people want and to hypothesize on why they want these things.

Disciplined Agile sales teams will consider the following strategies:

1. **Do away with sales commissions and sales quotas**. Although many sales people will not like this strategy, the fact is that sales commissions, and worse yet quarterly or annual sales quotas, will motivate dysfunctional behavior by your sales people. This includes selling customers things they may not need, selling them more than they need, or even selling them things that you don't actually have (yet). If you want to *Delight Customers* then your sales efforts should focus on doing what's right for the customer instead of what's profitable for the sales person.

2. **Sell what's on the truck**. This is an old sales adage that advises sales people to focus on selling what is actually available right now. When sales people promise new features that don't yet exist, or may not be viable, this can create havoc within the IT delivery teams. Schedules may be impacted to the point where previous promises to customers are put at risk due to refocusing on the new "fire drill" and you may discover that "simple features" that have been promised to a customer are significantly more expensive than you initially thought. If sales people are going to sell new things that don't yet exist, and it will occasionally happen, then they should first work with both the appropriate Product Management people (Chapter 5) and the IT delivery team to ensure that what

they're selling is both desirable and viable.

3. **Reward sales people for long-term, delighted customers.** Sales should be more consultative, measured by delivering great customer service rather than revenue generated. One option is to give sales people a base salary plus bonus based on customer reviews or a similar measure of customer delightedness. Another option is to also factor in the long-term profitability of the customer and more importantly how the sales person is contributing to growing business with that customer. This motivates sales people to focus on customer experience, which is much healthier for the long-term success of your DAE. Furthermore, rewarding sales people in a different manner than you reward others in the value stream, such as the people producing or supporting your offerings, can be demotivating.

4. **Enable salespeople to maximize time with customers.** You can't support your customers when you're at your desk doing paperwork. Automate away the non-value-added work as much as possible.

5. **Apply advanced analytics to establish prices in real time.** Your goal should be to obtain the highest yield possible from each transaction [DavenportHarris]. A perfect example of this is the way that Uber prices a fare – when demand goes up, perhaps due to poor weather or because it's rush hour, the price of a ride goes up. Uber sets prices in real time based on the current supply of drivers available in a given area and the demand of potential passengers.

6. **Tailor offerings to profitable customers.** An important way that you can *Delight Customers* is to tailor your offerings to better suit their needs. For example airlines regularly do this via their loyalty programs, offering "perks" such as seat upgrades, better food and drinks, valet parking, concierge services at the airport, and many other options to their frequent flyers in an effort to motivate them to continue flying regularly with the airline. Tailoring offerings to specific customers can require significant analytics to identify what the customer would potentially like as well as an understanding of the total cost structure of your value stream.

7. **Demand continuous delivery from IT.** When organizations are still taking a big release approach to their product line, think the quasi-annual Microsoft Office updates (such as Office 2013) of a few years ago, then customers will slow

down and even stop buying just before a major release because they would often prefer to get the new release. When the IT delivery team takes a continuous delivery approach, think Microsoft Office 365 which currently has weekly updates, then customers will not be motivated to wait for an upcoming release, thereby providing you with a steadier stream of incoming revenue. Continuous delivery approaches also tend to be easier on salespeople because they don't need to learn about, and track, the features provided by each major release.

Legal

 The aim of your Legal processes is to ensure that your organization works within the parameters of the law of any legal territory in which you operate. Your legal team will work closely with your procurement people, in many organizations Procurement is part of your overall legal efforts, on (Agile) contracts. They will also assist your people management team to ensure that their strategies reflect the local statutes and with your marketing team to guide what they're legally able to promise.

There is a very wide range of activities that your legal team will be involved with:

1. **Guide intellectual property (IP) management.** This includes the creation of patents, the filing of copyrights, and helping to navigate the international issues pertaining to such.
2. **Assist with organizational evolution.** In addition to organic evolution by creating and growing value streams, organizations may choose to evolve through merging with other organizations, acquiring other organizations, and selling portions of themselves that no longer fit in their enterprise portfolio. All of these activities require significant legal work.
3. **Provide legal guidance to others.** Your legal staff will regularly help teams and people within your organization to understand and navigate regulations in a pragmatic manner. They will also help to educate people in fundamental legal and ethical issues to enable better-informed decisions.
4. **Automate legal bureaucracy.** A 2016 study by Deloitte claims that artificial intelligence (AI) technologies are now being applied to automate a significant portion of legal work [Deloitte]. Increased automation enables your legal team to *Optimize Flow* and focus on leadership and coaching activities.

5. **Monitor the regulatory environment.** Your legal team will actively monitor the environment for new regulations and changes to existing regulations. They will work closely with your Control efforts to help keep them abreast of changes.

6. **Collaborate with regulators.** Large companies frequently work with regulators and legislators to explain their intentions and clear the way for work they want to do. For example, here in Canada disparate competitors such as Bell Canada, Corus Entertainment, and Shaw Media will regularly collaborate with their regulator, the Canadian Radio-television and Telecommunications Commission (CRTC) to provide practical inputs into regulations that affect them all.

Finance

 Your Disciplined Agile Finance efforts will focus on a collection of potentially competing goals, such as ensuring cash flow within your organization, ensuring your money is being spent well, taxes are minimized, spending is properly tracked and recorded, and legal financial reporting is being performed properly. All of this will be performed in a manner that is compliant with applicable financial regulations, such as Financial Accounting Standards Board (FASB) and International Accounting Standards Board (IASB) guidelines.

A Disciplined Agile approach to finance is based on the following philosophies:

1. **Spend the money wisely.** Your true goal should be to help your organization invest your revenue well, not just to set and monitor budgets. In other words, finance people must help others to make important decisions, not just "count the beans."

2. **Constrain teams with budgets, but don't hobble them.** A budget is the total sum of funds set aside for a given purpose, it is a ceiling on how much you're willing to spend on an idea. Financial constraints can motivate teams to be more creative and to focus on just the key aspects of a value stream. However, when teams have insufficient funding their ability to react to new opportunities will be greatly diminished.

3. **Distinguish between financial reporting and financial budgeting.** Financial reporting is often quarterly and annual, as per common legal requirements of publicly traded companies. Financial budgeting, on the other hand, can be on a schedule of your own choosing and does not need to be tied to the calendar.

4. **Prefer rolling wave budgeting over annual budgeting.** A

DAE must be able to respond rapidly to new opportunities and unpredictable events, but the annual budgeting approach was never designed to enable that. In the book *Beyond Budgeting* Jeremy Hope and Robin Fraser describe how to take a continuous approach to budgeting that enables you to invest revenue, control costs, and ensure you are moving in the right direction more effectively than traditional annual budgeting strategies ever did. The basic idea is to think through current expenditures in detail and future expenditures in less detail, monitoring both opportunities and challenges so that you can flexibly and sensibly direct funds where they are most needed today. Fundamentally, your knowledge about what your (potential) customers desire evolves continuously, so shouldn't your approach to finance match the realities that you face in the modern marketplace?

5. **Provide financial guidance to others**. Your financial staff will regularly help teams and people within your organization to understand the financial implications of their decisions. They will also help to educate people in the fundamentals of finance to enable them to make more informed decisions.

6. **Fund three growth horizons**. An important focus of your Finance efforts should be to enable the growth of value streams. Figure 6.4 depicts the Three Horizon Growth Model, each of which requires its own approach to finance [McKinsey]. Horizon 1 requires an operational mindset because the value streams in this horizon are mature and self-funding, requiring financial monitoring and perhaps guidance when important changes are made. Horizon 2 requires an entrepreneurial mindset and the value streams here may require investment funding to enable them to grow into Horizon 1. Value streams in the Horizon 2 state will require robust financial governance to keep them on track and in some cases to cull value streams that do not appear to be working out. Horizon 3 requires a venture capital mindset, requiring seed funding to initiate new value streams.

7. **Monitor the cash flow of value streams**. Finance people will collaborate with value stream leaders to provide guidance into their go-forward strategies. Sometimes a value stream needs to pivot, sell off the business, or simply end it before it goes too far into loss territory. You want to ensure that your incoming revenues are sufficient to fund the enterprise and to identify which of your value streams are healthy "going concerns."

8. **Prefer activity-based accounting over resource-based accounting.** With an activity-based approach you allocate the total costs to the value stream that drives those costs (and generates the revenue) so that you have a true picture of the financial benefits provided by the value stream. With resource-based accounting you allocate costs to functional areas such as IT or marketing, often treating them as an overhead instead of as a key part to your value stream(s).

> **Be Pragmatic About CapEx/OpEx**
> The capital expense (CapEx)/operating expense (OpEx) financial reporting model reflects 20th century thinking around physical assets and project-based accounting. It is important for organizations to track CapEx and OpEx for tax advantages and allocating costs appropriately to future periods. It doesn't fit well with Disciplined Agile strategies around experimentation, learning, and adaptability. If we're serious about being able to adapt to changing market conditions, it shouldn't matter what financial bucket the funding comes from. Nor do we want to divert valuable management resources away from adding value to our customers to play financial games moving money between artificial buckets. CapEx/OpEx issues are really financial report concerns, not budgeting concerns. Remember the DA principle of *Pragmatism*.

9. **Prefer team-based accounting over individual time tracking.** Tracking individuals' time with time tracking software can be very time consuming, and the data collected is usually not accurate. It can be incredibly difficult for team members to track how they spend their day in today's modern collaborative team environments. If the goal is to separate CapEx from OpEx there are much simpler ways to track this at the team level, such as setting reasonable ratios for how time is being spent, rather than individual timesheets.

10. **Automate, automate, automate.** As long as someone is typing financial data into a spreadsheet there is room for greater automation. In recent years great strides have been made in real-time financial reporting via business intelligence (BI) technologies feeding automated dashboards. Particularly important is cash-flow trend analysis to enable timely, fact-based discussions.

131

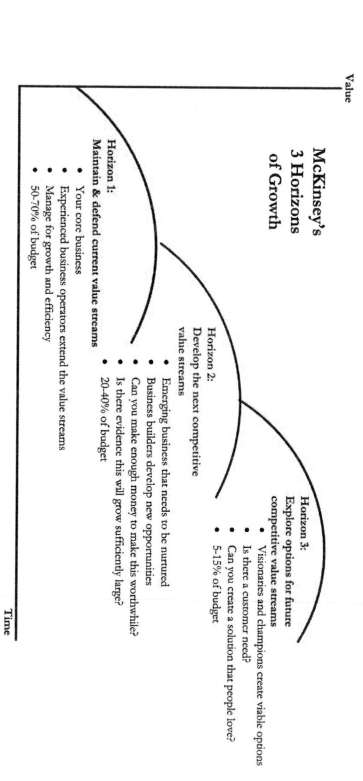

Figure 6.4. McKinsey's three-horizon growth model.

Value

McKinsey's
3 Horizons
of Growth

Horizon 1:
Maintain & defend current value streams

- Your core business
- Experienced business operators extend the value streams
- Manage for growth and efficiency
- 50-70% of budget

Horizon 2:
Develop the next competitive
value streams

- Emerging business that needs to be nurtured
- Business builders develop new opportunities
- Can you make enough money to make this worthwhile?
- Is there evidence this will grow sufficiently large?
- 20-40% of budget

Horizon 3:
Explore options for future
competitive value streams

- Visionaries and champions create viable options
- Is there a customer need?
- Can you create a solution that people love?
- 5-15% of budget

Time

An important observation of the Three-Horizon Growth Model of Figure 6.4 is that the time frames for all three horizons are shrinking. The implication is that you need to prove your value streams of Horizon 3 quicker, ideally via the Lean Startup-based Exploratory lifecycle described in Chapter 3. When in Horizon 2 your value streams need to become self-funding quicker, hence the need for the continuous delivery lifecycles also described in Chapter 3.

Control

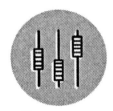

Your Control team, although some organizations adopt the Spotify term "control tribe", will collaborate closely with Finance and Legal. The aim is to monitor and guide teams, enabling them to succeed by removing or at least reducing any barriers that they may experience. To accomplish this your control team will:

1. **Coordinate organizational governance efforts**. In short, someone needs to govern the governors to ensure that your IT governance (Chapter 5), Financial Governance, People Management/Human Resource (HR) Governance strategies, and others are consistent and coherent.

2. **Identify mandatory regulations**. Your control tribe will work closely with Legal to identify applicable industry regulations. Note that regulations will vary by geographic territory and will evolve over time, so be prepared to do this work on an ongoing basis.

3. **Identify voluntary regulations**. Your organization may choose to willingly adopt Capability Maturity Model Integration (CMMI) guidance and even some of the International Organization for Standardization (ISO) regulations due to marketing reasons. Many customer organizations will only do business with companies who are compliant with certain industry regulations, insisting that their vendors are ISO 9003 or CMMI-3 compliant for example. As an aside, the DA framework not only exceeds the advice called out in CMMI it provides a more pragmatic approach to process maturity in our opinion [CMMI].

4. **Facilitate the development of compliancy strategies**. A key to the Disciplined Agile Control process blade is that your control team actively collaborates with the target audience to evolve your enterprise guidance, it doesn't dictate procedures from their ivory tower.

5. **Ensure regulatory compliancy**. This should be kept as light-weight as possible. A significant portion of regulatory compliancy

can often be automated. For example, automated regression testing often satisfies verification requirements; a combination of behavior-driven development (BDD) and test-driven development (TDD) provide traceability from requirements to design to code to tests; and continuous deployment (CD) strategies can provide evidence of separation of

> **Pragmatism Must Drive Compliancy**
> Be very careful how you choose to conform to regulatory guidance, particularly voluntary guidance. A pragmatic, light-weight approach is just as compliant as a heavy-weight approach, yet injects must less risk and cost.

concerns. Or, use of agile tools such as the Atlassian suite or Microsoft's Team Foundation Server (TFS) can also provide similar traceability. An important enabler of compliance is the education and coaching of people so that they understand the compliancy strategy in the first place

6. **Run internal audits**. The control team will be responsible for running internal audits to ensure compliancy, the goal being to ensure that a value stream or even a corporate division will pass an external audit.

Many of the strategies that we described in Chapter 5 regarding IT Governance apply to Control: Lead by example; prefer motivation over command and control; prefer enablement over audit; communicate continuously; streamline collaboration; be transparent; enable continuous improvement; consider both the long and short term; and take a holistic approach. Additionally, the following strategies enable a Disciplined Agile approach to Control:

1. **Ensure personal safety and experimentation**. Senior leadership needs to promote a "can do" and "no blame" culture where it is not only safe but highly desirable to learn via experimentation. Senior leadership should be there to help when things don't work out and to celebrate the learnings from both successes and failures.

2. **Promote self-organizing teams**. Senior leadership should push decision making authority down to the execution level, with teams being responsible for customer outcomes. An implication is that teams need fast access to resources and must be able to grow or shrink as needed, with senior leadership playing an enabling role in doing so. In a DAE, teams are not only allowed to self-organize they are pushed to

do so. Leaders should challenge local strategies and plans, motivating teams to improve and excel and to ensure risks are properly considered.

3. **Prefer guidelines over edicts.** Plans and procedures don't hold organizations together, instead clear purpose and values do. People are not going to read detailed procedures, and even if they do it's unlikely that they will follow them to the letter. With self-organizing teams leaders may fear that teams will get creative in some way and cause trouble, and to ease that fear you need to create clear and pragmatic guidelines within which people should operate.

4. **Create sandboxes.** Sandboxes are safe places for people to play, that have clear and reasonable boundaries with which teams can operate [SenseRespond]. Because sandbox boundaries can be hard to anticipate you will find that teams will often stumble across a prohibition or another team's boundary and will then have to work through what the boundaries and interfaces actually are.

5. **Mission command over rigid instructions.** There is a style of military leadership called "mission command" that defines the operational goals that a team is to achieve and then puts as much responsibility and authority into the hands of the team as possible [Bungay]. Mission command is based on several principles: Do not command more than necessary, or plan beyond foreseeable circumstances; Communicate to every team as much of the higher intent as is necessary to achieve the purpose; and ensure that everyone retains freedom of decision within bounds (their sandboxes).

6. **Collect actionable metrics.** A good metric provides insight, it motivates you to change your behavior. If you don't use a metric to improve or make better decisions then it is a vanity metric and therefore overhead [LeanAnalytics]. BUT, at the same time you can't manage solely by the numbers. Instead use metrics to identify where you need to have conversations about what is(n't) happening.

7. **Prefer real-time automated intelligence.** Throughout this book we've discussed concepts such as development intelligence, operational intelligence, and IT intelligence. The real goal of course is business intelligence (BI) where you can quickly identify emerging trends, make predictions, and take prompt action in an informed manner. Effective BI can also provide an "early warning" strategy for identifying potential

marketplace changes. Will you always get it right? No, but you will make better decisions more often than if you didn't have BI. An important nuance is that the purpose of measurement is to reduce uncertainty, it isn't to gain certainty.

8. **Measure customer outcomes**. A DAE measures outcomes, not outputs because you cannot guide effectively without confronting the facts. Key performance indicators (KPIs) such as total customer profitability, cycle time, attrition, and market share are all outcome based. Because it is difficult to forecast accurately, your predictive KPIs should be quoted in ranges that reflect the uncertainty of the base data.

9. **Manage for throughput over utilization**. As Tom DeMarco recommends in his book *Slack*, if you want to maximize the throughput of a team (and thereby reduce time to respond to opportunities) you need to have slack time built into the way that you work. When people are fully utilized they are more likely to become bottlenecks for the people they are supposed to collaborate with, and they have no capacity to quickly respond to a new opportunity when it arises [DeMarco]. The principles are to *Optimize Flow* and *Be Awesome*, not *Fully Utilize Staff* and *Be Busy*.

10. **Transparency for everyone enables control**. Allowing everyone to see the same information at the same time will enable people to ask the right questions and make the right decisions. This includes giving people access to strategic, competitive, and market information that would have only been available to executives in traditional organizations. How can keeping people ignorant be a good idea? Furthermore, keep numbers in their raw state – when you "fudge them" or modify them to look good you reduce the opportunity to have open and honest discussions about what is really going on. The good news is that when everyone sees the numbers at the same time there is little opportunity for people to fudge the numbers.

11. **Provide audit guidance to teams**. People fear being audited, rightly or wrongly. Although audits can be a great learning opportunity for teams to identify where they've missed addressing important risks this is often overshadowed by the threat that they will get in trouble and may even be punished. A Disciplined Agile control team will provide pragmatic advice to teams about what they need to do to pass audits, ideally providing real-world examples of how teams passed

audits within your organization in the past.

12. **Govern by exception.** Executives should look for exceptions or unusual patterns and trends that might reflect changes in customer behavior or poor behavior on the part of teams.

Procurement

 The aim of the Procurement process blade, sometimes called vendor management, is to help obtain products and services from other organizations. To do this your procurement team will collaborate with other parts of the organization to understand their procurement needs (if any), identify potential vendors that can fulfill those needs, and work with Legal to develop appropriate contracts. Organizationally your procurement team is often part of, or at least closely related to, your legal team.

The following strategies enable a Disciplined Agile approach to Procurement:

1. **Collaborate closely with the actual people for which you procure.** Very often the team that requires a product or service be procured for them will have a very good understanding of good options, and sometimes the best option, available. Listen to them and trust them.

> **Are You Optimizing Procurement at the Expense of the Whole?**
> We have seen many situations where Procurement is far from agile. The movement to reduce the number of "preferred" vendors in the interest of bargaining, risk management, pricing consistency, and less paperwork often leads to significant inefficiencies during contract execution. The large preferred vendors often have to subcontract the work to smaller consultancies who have the actual skills, leading to a much higher rate than if procurement contracted with the smaller company to begin with. We also often see staffing of unqualified, poorly skilled people because procurement went with the lowest bidder or because the vendor could place anyone they wanted into a team under a general services contract.

2. **Work with the right vendors.** Many organizations make the mistake of working with a limited number of vendors, often to simplify procurement. But, if you want the best fit, then you really need to work with a range of vendors. Larger companies tend to offer commodity services and products, smaller companies are more leading edge but may not have the capacity for larger efforts,

and independents are often experts in a specific topic.

3. **Build partnerships**. When it comes to procured services, vendor staff will often be a critical part of a value stream. So treat them as such and embed them as closely as you can. Scott once worked with a company where the integration of full-time employees (FTEs) and contractors was so good they challenged him to identify which company each person on the team actually worked for – he couldn't do it. Note that some countries, particularly the US, have specific laws that limit how you are able to treat contractors and consultants and may even put an upper limit on how long they may work for you.

4. **Prefer context-sensitive contracts**. Although this shouldn't have to be said, we've seen far too many organizations where their procurement team appears to have a "one size fits all" mentality. The point is that a multi-million dollar services contract will be a bit more detailed than a contract for two-day workshop. A contract for Agile services should reflect how an agile team works whereas a contract for traditional services should reflect how a traditional team works. Use the right contract for what you are trying to procure – *Context counts*.

5. **Beware the extremes**. When it comes to comparing vendors based on cost, which is a questionable strategy at best, our advice is that the vendors in the middle are likely your best bets. Our experience is that lowest bidder will very likely produce low quality or will nickle-and-dime you via their change management strategy whereas the highest bidder either doesn't want your business to begin with, aren't very streamlined in the way that they work, or in some cases really are the very best and know what they're worth.

6. **Prefer flexible funding contracts over fixed-bid contracts**. Fixed-bid tends to focus on initial price, thus promoting a lowest-bid mindset which generally leads to trouble. Systems thinking tells us to end the practice of awarding business on the basis of price tag and instead minimize total cost [Deming] (or better yet net value received). Fixed price contracts tend to be a worst-case scenario for all parties involved.

7. **Prefer incremental delivery contracts over big-bang contracts**. The larger the contract, the greater the risk. To remove that risk, when you can, break a large contract into small incremental deliverables. You reduce the cost of delay by doing so [Reinertsen], introduce opportunities for learning and adjusting your strategy, and increase overall transparency.

8. **Prefer outcome-based contracts over feature-based contracts**.

Just like your internal metrics should be outcome-focused so should your contracts. There is no guarantee that the features you defined up front will be what customers actually want [BRUF]. Instead define contracts in terms of outcomes – increased sales, increased customer retention, customer growth, and so on. Effective contracts define a set of outcomes to achieve, a set of constraints, and give the team the freedom to work within that sandbox.

9. **Avoid detailed contractual processes**. Large amounts of up-front planning tends to increase risk in complex situations [Reinertsen]. Worse yet, detailed contractual processes tend to favor incumbents and large service providers (as opposed to the right vendors), they inhibit transparency (rarely exploring how a vendor will provide a service), they are inaccurate (everyone tends to be overly optimistic), and they often ignore outcomes in favor of outputs [LeanEnterprise].

10. **Monitor fulfillment of contracts**. Past performance is critical input into determining whether to award new work to a vendor, which is a significant motivator to act as a good partner right now. Just like regular retrospectives to identify potential improvements works well for solution delivery teams, the same technique can be applied to identify how well a contract is being fulfilled and more importantly how to address any problems you're currently experiencing.

Business Operations

 The Business Operations process blade focuses on the activities required to provide services to customers and to support your products. The implementation of business operations will vary by value stream, in a bank retail account services is implemented in a very different manner than brokerage services for example. Business operations includes help desk and support services (integrated in with IT support where appropriate) as well as any technical sales support activities such as training, product installation, and product customization. As you can imagine close collaboration with both your Sales and Marketing efforts is required to successfully *Delight Customers*.

Figure 6.5 indicates that Business Operations is an important part of the overall set of interactions that your organization has with customers.

Figure 6.5. Customer interaction with your organization.

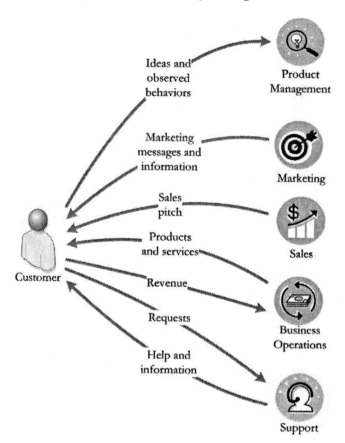

Now We Just Need to Get There

This chapter explored what a DAE is, describing the major process blades within your organization and how they work within a DAE. Some areas within your organization will need to make very few changes whereas others will have significant changes to make. Every organization is different, hence the DA framework provides you with choices.

The next two chapters focus on organizational transformation strategies and how to shift into a continuous improvement strategy respectively. Your first instinct is to treat this effort like a project that you slog through for several months and then viola!, you're suddenly a DAE. The reality is that becoming a DAE is a journey, not a destination.

7 A DISCIPLINED APPROACH TO AGILE TRANSFORMATIONS

"Agile transformations" are all the rage these days. Morphing your organization from a traditional structure and culture to one exhibiting true business agility is very hard and takes a long time. Hiring inexperienced change agents, using an unstructured or waterfall approach, and expecting to be "done" in a short period of time are patterns that typically fail and any improvements seen are often not sustained over time. We, as an industry, need to do better.

In this chapter we focus on strategies for your initial transformation to a model that supports true business agility at the team, IT, and enterprise levels.

A Multi-Pronged Transformation Strategy

Over time the focus of your work will change. Figure 7.1. depicts the relative focus of your transformation and improvement efforts over time – your actual approach will vary based on how willing people are to learn and how much help that they need in order to do so. It shows how you'll have a heavy investment in coaching, education, and training early on but how you eventually shift over into self-service strategies such as experimental learning and CoPs/guilds.

Figure 7.1 Focus of the relative transformation effort over time.

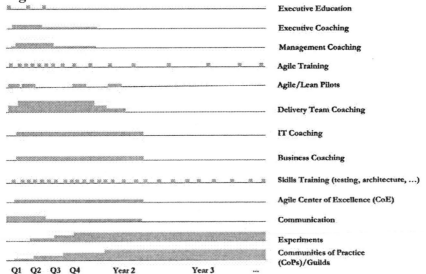

Your focus will vary over time in the following areas:

1. **Executive education**. You should invest your initial effort on achieving alignment with your executive stakeholders on the vision for your transformation. We have found that a one-day executive workshop is extremely valuable to ensure that your senior leadership understands what enterprise agility means, what an agile organization looks like, as well as the change management approach to effective and sustainable agility. The initial executive education may be broken

> **Leaders Must Lead.**
> Jon Smart of Barclays UK has said that "Management must enthusiastically champion the change, not merely tolerate it". If anyone doubts leadership's support or if there is belief that the change is temporary, your transformation WILL fail.

up into several sessions for leaders at various levels of the organization. Importantly, this education needs to be for all IT stakeholders including enterprise groups such as Project Management Offices (PMOs) and Enterprise Architecture, as well as business stakeholders. We have seen transformation failures that could be traced back to not engaging business executives from the very beginning.

2. **Executive coaching**. Executive involvement does not end with initial education. As key stakeholders, or what we might call the "Chief Product Owners" of the transformation initiative, a small but ongoing commitment of time is required to help steer your adoption team. What are the key organizational impediments that must be addressed for enterprise agility to be achievable? What metrics should we focus on to measure the success if the transformation? Your executive coach will help you with these decisions. In addition, effective and transparent communication at all levels is important to minimize anxiety related to the uncertainty of change. It is very, very important that senior leadership is seen as a positive change agent.

3. **Middle-management coaching**. It is also important to include middle/team management in your coaching. These folks are too often neglected, yet we have seen them to be the single biggest potential source of passive (or even active) resistance to the transformation, as they may perceive their

142

jobs and livelihoods to be on the line. The timing of middle management coaching is dependent on your desire to realign your organizational structure.

4. **Agile training**. Some of your teams may have had some basic agile or Scrum training. However, a disciplined approach to agile in the enterprise is not covered by this type of training. You will want to educate your teams on the realities of enterprise agile development and equip them with strategies that can help them to maximize their agility for the unique context of your organization and its IT initiatives.

5. **Agile/lean pilot teams**. As we describe later in this chapter, simultaneous with the top-down transformation education and coaching, you will want to demonstrate successful agile delivery at the team level.

6. **Delivery team coaching**. Team coaches can help increase your chances of success on your first agile/lean initiatives. Team coaching will be particularly intense in the early stages of your adoption. A coach will typically get a pilot team started, coaching them through the first phases and iterations of their initiative. Once a team gets going, the coach can turn to starting up another pilot team, regularly circling back to other pilot teams in progress.

7. **IT coaching**. Your Enterprise and Team Coaches will work with your enterprise groups with which your pilot teams need to collaborate to ensure that these groups understand how to effectively engage with the teams in an agile manner. This coaching includes educating and negotiating change with all IT stakeholders so that they understand the new, more agile and nimble, ways in which we expect them to interact with your new agile teams. We like to call this "greasing the skids" for the teams. For example, you may wish to work with your governance bodies to implement a more streamlined business case approach. Or work with the Enterprise Architecture group to streamline or eliminate the need for upfront architectural designs. When the scope of your transformation is truly enterprise-wide (as we discussed in Chapter 6) then this coaching would also extend beyond IT groups to business enterprise groups such as marketing, legal, and procurement.

8. **Business coaching**. An important part of optimizing your whole organization, not just IT, is to help the business to understand how to maximize the new benefits of business agility available to them with agile delivery teams at their

disposal. They will want to become more agile themselves, learning to continuously plan and flow work to stable teams, moving away from elaborate business cases, annual funding and budgeting rituals.

9. **Skills training**. Periodically you will want to invest in specialized training in particular areas, such as architecture, product ownership, and agile testing practices. You will likely need to have several agile teams up and running to justify filling a workshop for these specialties. With the over-specialization of skills that are typical within traditional teams, when people first join an agile team it's common to discover that they need training in the skills that they're missing.

10. **Agile Center of Excellence (CoE)**. To drive your agile transformation effort you will want to establish a CoE. The purpose is not to dictate agile practices but to guide the overall transformation effort, following the suggested approach described in this chapter. Figure 7.2 shows an example of how an Agile CoE can guide all stakeholders in effective adoption of agile and lean principles. The CoE team members are considered mentors for your agile adoption for all stakeholders, including your delivery teams, the IT enterprise groups, and business stakeholders.

11. **Communication**. Jon Smart, when describing lessons learned from Barclays' agile journey is fond of saying "communicate, communicate, communicate" (with emphasis). Fear and uncertainty have been the downfall of many a change initiative. You need to have an explicit communication strategy to engage leaders to help cascade communications down and across your organization. A common mistake is to take an IT centric approach to communication. Business stakeholders need to be equally included in your communications plans. They are the key stakeholders after all.

12. **Experiments**. Maximizing your effectiveness with agility is a learning endeavor. Using the Lean Change management technique that we describe later in this chapter, every process improvement that we make is considered an experiment. Incrementally introducing these small changes that minimize organizational disruption while constantly making improvements is an effective way to effect sustainable change.

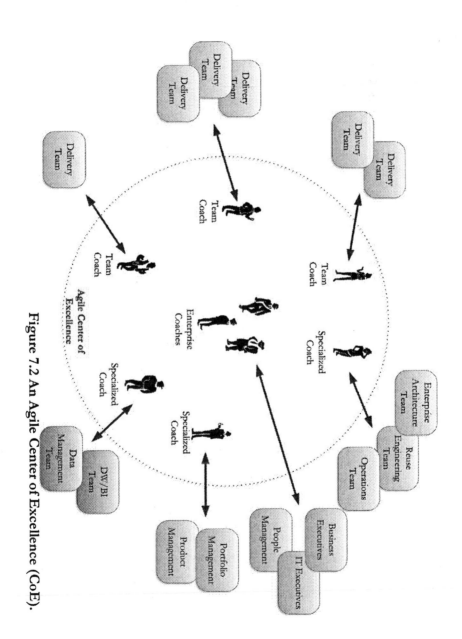

Figure 7.2 An Agile Center of Excellence (CoE).

13. Communities of Practice (CoPs)/Guilds. A CoP, also known as a Guild (after Medieval Guilds which specialized in a craft such as Blacksmithing), exists to further the science or craft of a particular discipline such as agile requirements modeling, agile coaching, or automated testing. Unlike CoEs which are typically staffed full-time (at least for some period), CoPs are staffed part-time by practitioners, usually on a voluntary basis – think of it as an "internal user group" of people coming together to help each other learn. It is common however for one or more members of your CoE, often a coach, to sit in on your CoPs to represent your organization's established approach, as well as to harvest new proven techniques from the CoPs. It is best to initially staff your CoPs with your internal experts, along with expert coaches in the particular discipline focused on by each CoPs. Over time these leaders should rotate out of the CoP so that others can take their turn. It is the responsibility of the CoP to not only contribute to furthering their "craft", establishing techniques, tools and practices that make sense for your organization, but to also ensure that these learnings and standards are effectively communicated across your organization.

Transformations are Hard

We all know that change is hard. Not only is it hard to effect, but it is hard to sustain. In fact, change efforts have a lousy record. Standish Group cites the average success of change initiatives at 35% [ChaosReport].

We've seen transformations fail to meet expectations for the following reasons:

- Believing that transformation timelines are

measured in months rather than years

- Not having management support from the very top
- Pushing change on people instead of finding ways to help them to pull improvements into their teams
- Inadequate and ineffective communication
- Lack of trust due to lack of transparency in all things related to the change initiative
- Inadequate investment in training and coaching
- Lack of expectation that mentors, coaches and practitioners should have invested significant time in worthwhile certifications representative of real and diversified experience
- Insufficient support, authority and/or courage to execute necessary change related to organizational structure, work spaces, governance, human resources practices, finance, and other aspects of organizational change

Your transformation is unique to your organization – You will need to steer your own journey. Sometimes you will have the opportunity to "off-road" and cut a new path, but very often you will go down a combination of existing paths that others have built for you. You should leverage the experiences of others as much as you can. Whether you are starting your change initiative from scratch, or continuing your change journey, you should use an appropriate change management framework. There are many to choose from such as ADKAR, Kotter, and Lewen to name a few. Later in this chapter we share our preferred approach to steering transformation using Lean Change which incorporates a blend of structured approaches such as those listed with lean concepts of experiment-driven change.

Invest in Your People

There is an overused phase that says "time is money". Agile has been around officially since the Agile Manifesto was crafted in 2001, and unofficially for years before that. Organizations that have not yet adopted agile and lean, let alone deriving significant benefits from it are, it must be said, laggards in the agile adoption curve. The best way to catch up is to apply three accelerators, namely training, certification, and coaching.

Training to Get You Going

While the most cost effective way of learning might be through reading, it may be more expedient to bring teams together in a workshop setting to share experiences and receive context driven face-to-face training. Certified Disciplined Agile workshops are rich in exercises and discussions focused on challenges and perceived impediments to successful agile adoption and how they may be overcome. Of course training is no guarantee that every attendee has actually learned something. This leads us to validation of learning via certification.

Certification to Validate Learning

Many people have developed a cynical view of agile certification, and given the various scams they have good reason. Some certifications are "earned" simply by attending a workshop. The Disciplined Agile Consortium was formed to create a reputable certification program that can be trusted by employers and that is challenging and worthwhile for Disciplined Agile practitioners.

The program was designed with several principals in mind. First and foremost, a certification must provide value to the person being certified. This value comes from learning new and valuable strategies during the process of earning the certification as well as greater employability resulting from the certification. Of course there are always limits to the value of any certification. Certifications must be earned and the effort required to earn the certification must be commensurate with the value provided. Certifications must also be respectable. The fact that you have to do some work to earn them is a welcome

Why Disciplined Agile Consortium (DAC) certification is different:

- There is no requirement to attend an expensive course to be certified. DAC recognizes that sufficient knowledge can be obtained from self-study. An inexpensive test is all that is required to prove sufficient knowledge

- While some certification plans require no actual experience, or worse only their proprietary method experience, DAC recognizes experience from any mainstream agile method. DAC's philosophy is inclusive.

- DAC requires references for experience in the field and *all* candidates' references are indeed checked.

- Continuous education is expected and tracked for certification renewals. Disciplined Agile continues to evolve with our industry.

difference from other agile certifications. Certification is worthwhile if it is part of your learning process. However, learning is not an event but instead an ongoing effort. The implication is that once you have earned your certification you must continue working to keep your skills up to date. Lastly, certified professionals have a responsibility to share knowledge.

Figure 7.3 The Disciplined Agile Certification program.

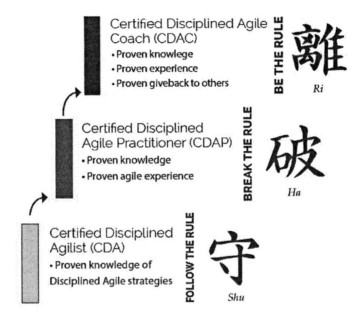

Measuring your Adoption with Certification

There are many ways to measure your successful agile adoption. One of these is to assess the degree to which your teams have been certified, and hence are equipped with the knowledge and experience to sustain and further grow your agile transformation. For instance, you could ask:

- How well do my team members understand agile principles and the strategies available to them for optimizing agile and lean for their context? Those with the CDA designation have proven via a challenging test that they are aware of their options.
- How experienced are my teams actually applying these principles and have my teams' members developed a more advanced understanding of disciplined agile strategies? The CDAP designation requires that certified agilists have two years of

practical experience on agile teams, with checked references, and have passed a more difficult test on agile strategies.

- Do we have internal coaching capability to grow agile adoption in our organization in order to guide existing and new teams to assure successful execution? The CDAC designation demonstrates that certified coaches have deep experience and understanding of the rich Disciplined Agile framework. Their certification application requires a board review with a DA Fellow.

These measures clearly aren't an indication of specific agile benefits delivered, but they do show the degree to which your organization has the knowledge and experience to help achieve better agile results.

Coaching to Success

We like to refer to coaching as "success assurance". Having a coach working side-by-side with your agile teams as well as management is the best way to ensure that your adoption will be successful. Making it truly sustainable requires organizational transformation which we discuss later in more detail. There are several benefits to coaching:

1. **Building self-awareness**. An important principle of agile is that teams should be self-organizing. Teams should not be forced to follow a prescribed process, rather they should be permitted to adapt their own process as befits their unique context. Teams are best suited to decide what should be done, by whom, and when. Retrospectives are a common mechanism whereby teams reflect and self-improve in order to improve their delivery effectiveness and efficiency. However, for teams new to agile and lean a lack of self-awareness regarding the vast array of potential strategies available to them can limit the effectiveness of their own process improvement. An experienced coach has seen dozens or even hundreds of other similar situations and can provide pros and cons of various issues that teams and individuals face at first.

2. **Success assurance**. It is really important on your early agile teams to demonstrate success. There is a saying in the agile world it is important to "fail fast" or better yet learn fast. The principle is to have the courage to experiment, learn, and adapt. Failure is embraced as a learning opportunity. The principle is sound, and failing in the small is ok, but failing with your initial agile teams in the large could jeopardize your entire agile rollout. Agile coaches will certainly have had their share of failures in the past and will (hopefully) have learned from these experiences. Like a good

consultant, you expect a coach to recognize patterns of potential problems and steer the team towards successful strategies. Combining the experience of a good agile coach with the reference framework of process choices from the Disciplined Agile framework greatly increases your chances of succeeding earlier rather than failing fast.

3. **Accelerating your agile adoption**. It takes time for teams and individuals to learn how to work well together. Coaching can accelerate the process of learning and thus help to greatly improve the team's throughput and quality much quicker than waiting for them to figure things out on their own. Getting results quicker is certainly a business justification for the expense of a coach.

A serious problem in the agile community right now is that people with limited agile experience, especially at the enterprise coaching level, are quick to call themselves "Enterprise" or "Transformation" Coaches. This happens because they're being hired by organizations that don't know what to look for in a good coach. We have found that the features that make a Disciplined Agile (DA) coach effective include:

1. **People skills**. First and foremost, effective DA coaches need solid people skills. They need to be prepared to work with a wide range of people coming from different backgrounds, with different learning preferences, and with different learning goals. As a result DA coaches need to be emotionally intelligent, empathetic, patient, respectful, and open-minded.

2. **Experience**. Good coaches understand the situation that you face, and more importantly understand how to guide you to tailor your strategy. Effective coaches have many data points from their experiences over the years, and as such they can recognize patterns quickly and provide appropriate advice to those who are coaching. We've seen people who are very good agile coaches for small, co-located teams get into serious trouble the first time they need to deal with scaling factors such as large team size, geographic distribution, or regulatory compliance. We've also seen good development team coaches flounder when they first start to address, in a meaningful way, the Agile IT issues faced by organizations applying agile across their entire IT department. Extend to this the need to coach outside of IT in areas such as marketing, control, and procurement, and they find themselves quickly out of their depth. This is one of the reasons why we suggest that Transformation coaches be Certified Disciplined Agile Coaches (CDACs) as they need significant

experience and knowledge to be successful. The Project Management Institute (PMI) has come a long way in adopting agile approaches to project management. As such the PMI-ACP is a good complementary or preparatory certification to DA. The implication is that when you're hiring a coach, make sure they've worked in environments similar to yours. Otherwise you run the risk of paying for their learning experiences. Having said that, a coach who has also worked in a very different environment than yours may bring ideas and experiences from outside of your industry into your environment.

3. **Pragmatism**. As we like to say, DA is pragmatic agile. Effective DA coaches are willing and able to work closely with the people that they're coaching, providing practical advice that they follow themselves. They also like to have real-time measures that reveal how their team(s) are doing, enabling them to make fact-based suggestions to help their teams. Pragmatic coaches understand that the ideal conditions that agile purists describe may not be realistic for your company, and they are willing to be flexible in customizing an agile approach that makes sense not only for your organization but for each team.

4. **Knowledge**. It's reasonable to expect a DA coach to be very knowledgeable about DA and agile in general. Development team coaches are at least Certified Disciplined Agile Practitioners (CDAPs) and better yet CDACs. Transformation coaches, who coach an organization's executive team through the process of transitioning to agile, should be CDACs.

5. **Skill**. Development team coaches must be skilled in fundamental agile techniques such as regression testing, continuous integration (CI), iteration/sprint planning, look-ahead modelling and planning, requirements envisioning, and many more. A good team coach should also be skilled in "advanced" agile techniques such as test-driven development (TDD), behavior driven development (BDD), and continuous deployment. Transformation coaches should be skilled in organizational change management as well as the fundamentals of IT-level activities such as enterprise architecture, data management, operations, portfolio management, and others.

6. **Leadership**. In addition to solid people skills, good coaches must have leadership skills too, as they need to be adept at convincing people to follow their advice. Team coaches will often be Team Leads, or at least be working closely with the Team Lead, to help lead the team in making the "hard decisions"

required to successfully learn the agile mindset.

7. **Flexibility**. A fundamental concept of the DA framework is that you need to tailor it to meet the needs that you face. The implication is that DA coaches need to be agile to go beyond the advice in prescriptive methods such as Scrum or SAFe. Instead of working from a prescriptive playbook, DA coaches will leverage DA's goal-driven strategy to help guide teams make process-oriented and organization-oriented choices that are right for them. In short, just because someone has several years of Scrum coaching doesn't necessarily mean that you can count on them having the background to be a good DA coach; they may only understand Scrum strategies and not the full range of agile and lean strategies supported by the DA framework.

A Transformation Roadmap

Every transformation is unique so it would be wrong to depict a specific transformation roadmap applicable to your specific situation. However, at Scott Ambler + Associates we use a repeatable pattern or roadmap which we adapt for the size and context of the organization. Figure 7.4 depicts an example of what a roadmap might look like. Note that this is *just an example*. In reality your initial initiative will very likely be longer than 6 months. However, it is expected over that time that internal enablement of Enterprise and Team Coaches occurs through mentoring from external coaches if you use them.

We typically have a part-time Executive/Enterprise Coach paired with one or more Team Coaches. We actually prefer the term Enterprise over Executive Coach as, while much work is indeed working with the executives, this coach also works with the managers, as well your enterprise groups such as Enterprise Architecture, Release Management, Data, PMOs etc. As well, an important part of Enterprise Coaching is working with your business stakeholders. We recommend a multi-pronged approach:

- **Executive leadership**. Start with a short assessment to understand the context and come up with a realistic roadmap for the transformation initiative. Then provide a one-day workshop for the Executive to start the initiative. Coaching part-time then continues over a longer period of time to guide the transformation. Your executive leaders are the ultimate Product Owners for the initiative so you will need some regular time with them.

- **Functional/team management**. It is important that the managers of your new teams understand their new role as a manager of agile and lean teams. They should understand basic Disciplined Agile principles as well as receive some Functional Manager training. It is important to understand that you need to have well designed agile teams before beginning this training as the mix of managers to teams may change as part of the Transformation work.

> **Team Coaches as Team Leads.** A variation of the Team Coach role is to have the Team Coach also fulfill the Team Lead role on one of your delivery teams. Some organizations find it easier to justify the investment in a coach if they are also providing hands-on delivery. The compromise is that there are limitations on the number of teams that a Team Coach can kick start and coach if part of their time is dedicated to team leadership.

- **Business stakeholders**.
  Every team needs a Product Owner (PO), and there will be other business stakeholders (such as subject matter experts (SMEs) and Business Analysts) that need to understand the new agile way of working with the teams. So early in your initiative you should schedule PO training.

- **Teams**. You will need one or more Team Coaches to incrementally enable your new agile and lean teams. The pattern we recommend is some initial training followed by kicking off a team with a short Inception phase. Then the coach guides the team through a number of iterations to reinforce the principles learned. Simultaneously the coach can start the process of training and kick starting another team.

The overall transformation work using the *Lean Change* management approach described below will help you address your current organizational impediments to agility. With assistance from your Enterprise Coach, you will likely identify many potential areas for improvement, known in Lean Change as insights. Note that what is described below are just examples of the types of changes you *may* identify as priorities depending on your appetite for change and the realities of how you currently delivery IT solutions.

- **Organizational design**. It is very likely that your current organizational structure, job profiles, and mix of skills will need rebalancing based on your new delivery models. This will likely mean that you will need to engage your People Management team on matters such as job profiles and compensation models. Some organizations have more appetite for this type of change than others.

- **Team design.** An agile principle is to have cross functional teams wherein the team members have all the skills to get the job done without relying on people outside the team. Part of a transformation typically includes designing longer-term stable, cross functional teams.

- **Workspace/facilities design.** Look for opportunities to collocate your teams into common work areas. This may require working with your facilities department to design new working areas. If this is not possible, or only partially attainable, you'll need to make sure that you're not only providing the best possible tools for remote/distributed collaboration, but also providing some basic training on the mindset and behavioral changes that are necessary in order for distributed/dispersed collaboration to be effective[7].

- **Adoption of metrics.** It is difficult to understand if you are improving if you do not institute a minimal set of metrics as a baseline early in your initiative. Your Enterprise Coach will help you design the appropriate set of metrics.

- **Refinement of existing governance.** If you are a traditional organization it is likely that your current governance is not currently conducive to guiding agile teams. You will want to institute a more agile and lean flavor to your governance to cut down on the bureaucracy while maintaining sufficient oversight.

- **Addressing planning and budgeting.** You may wish to consider working with Finance to adopt modern ideas such as rolling wave planning, and those described in *Beyond Budgeting* in lieu of the more traditional annual planning ritual [HopeFraser]. Traditional practices such as detailed time tracking can be abandoned in favor of simplified tracking techniques.

---

[7] There's an extensive list of remote collaboration tools at http://www.collaborationsuperpowers.com/remote/

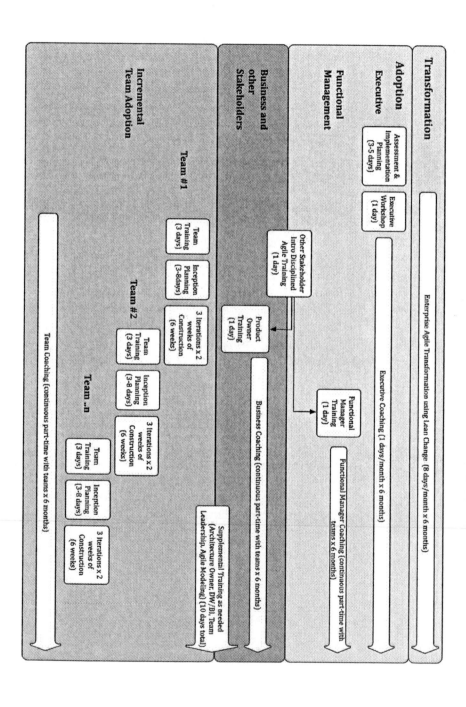

Figure 7.4 An example of a Transformation & Adoption Roadmap

A Lean Change Approach to Agile Transformations

We have described above typical example roadmaps and the mix of work that occurs over a multi-year transformation. But how is this change effected? You will need to use some sort of change management framework to plan, organize, and facilitate this change. For enterprise agile transformations, we use an approach largely based upon the works of Jeff Anderson [LeanChange1], Jason Little [LeanChange2], and others when we engage with organizations for their agile transformations. In this chapter we provide an overview of the approach that we have used over and over again for companies large and small around the world.

Start by developing, and agreeing to, your vision for your transformation efforts. Following an initial assessment, we start our transformation engagements by running several workshops to create a Vision with senior management regarding what we plan to accomplish during the engagement. The tool we prefer to use to capture the Vision is called a Change Canvas as depicted in Figure 7.5. The bottom of the sample canvas shows a Kanban board for visualizing and tracking the actual changes in progress. This canvas is created in a collaborative fashion with senior leadership, brainstorming each category in the canvas. Questions we would ask: Why are we doing this? What is the business urgency for this initiative? What time and budget are we each prepared to commit to its success? What is the end-state that we expect for a given timeline (in this case for the year 2017). Are there measurable benefits that we can expect to achieve? This canvas can be created in a couple of hours, and we recommend posting it on a very large poster in public areas. Transparency is your friend. This Vision becomes the beacon for all your transformation activity, and all people at all levels of the organization need to read it.

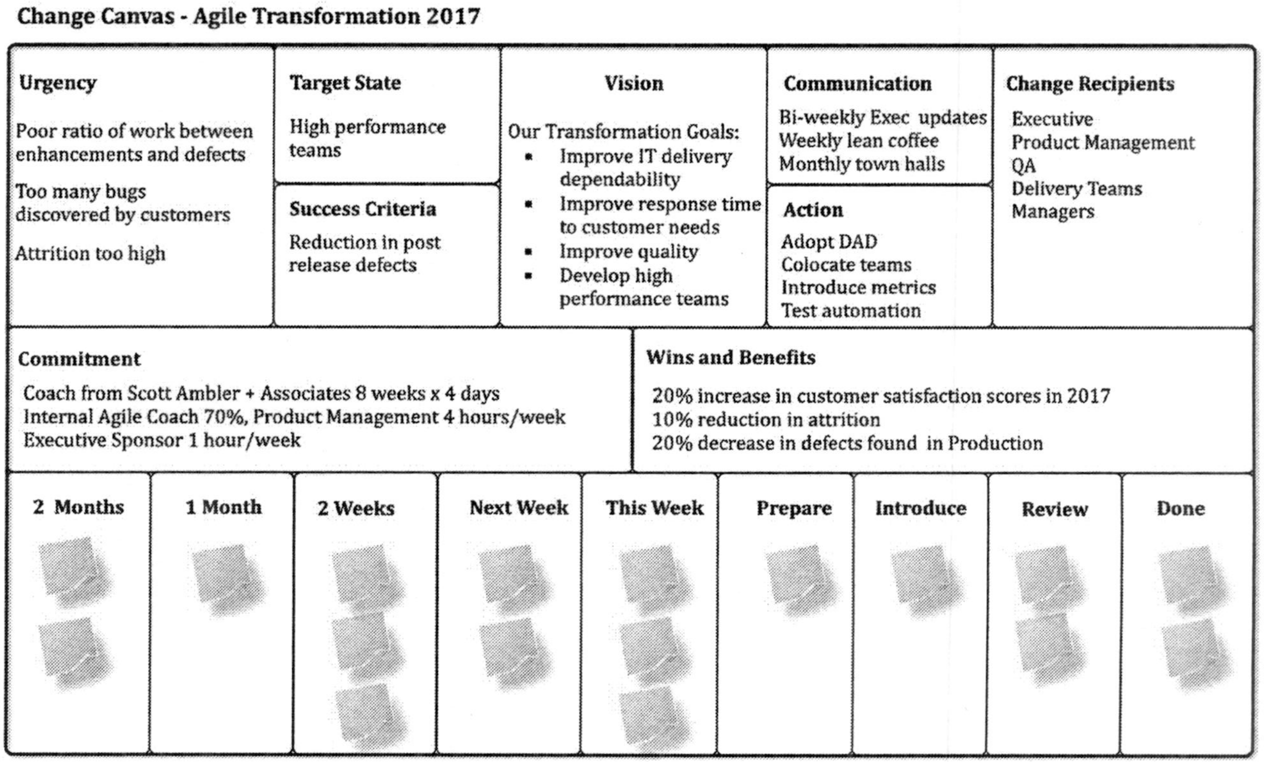

Change Canvas - Agile Transformation 2017

Urgency	Target State	Vision	Communication	Change Recipients
Poor ratio of work between enhancements and defects	High performance teams	Our Transformation Goals:	Bi-weekly Exec updates	Executive
Too many bugs discovered by customers		• Improve IT delivery dependability	Weekly lean coffee	Product Management
Attrition too high	**Success Criteria**	• Improve response time to customer needs	Monthly town halls	QA
	Reduction in post release defects	• Improve quality		Delivery Teams
		• Develop high performance teams	**Action**	Managers
			Adopt DAD	
			Colocate teams	
			Introduce metrics	
			Test automation	

Commitment

Coach from Scott Ambler + Associates 8 weeks x 4 days
Internal Agile Coach 70%, Product Management 4 hours/week
Executive Sponsor 1 hour/week

Wins and Benefits

20% increase in customer satisfaction scores in 2017
10% reduction in attrition
20% decrease in defects found in Production

2 Months	1 Month	2 Weeks	Next Week	This Week	Prepare	Introduce	Review	Done

Figure 7.5. Example of a Change Canvas for an Agile

You also want to identify the guiding principles for your transformation. During the initial stage of a transformation engagement we conduct executive and management educational workshops to provide overviews of what agile is and what fundamental changes are required to become a lean enterprise that is enabled to properly exhibit business and IT agility. We contrast what, in the past were considered "best practices" to the realities of what modern organizations need to do in order to be competitive and agile. For instance, it is commonly understood now that stable teams are typically far more productive than teams that are newly assembled for a project. Additionally, it is very costly and time consuming for a new team to evolve into a high performance team [Tuckman]. With a common baseline of understanding agile, a vision for the transformation, and guiding principles we can then strategize on what we are trying to achieve and what needs to be done. In a few short workshops we develop a common understanding of the current state and culture of the organization and the target state that we are collectively moving towards. A typical artifact created during these initial planning workshops would be the organization's guiding principles for their agile transformation. We use a Moving From/Moving To tool to ensure that all of management agree to these guiding principles. An example is shown in Figure 7.6.

Figure 7.6. An example of a Moving From/To chart to capture your guiding principles.

On our Journey towards Enterprise Agility we will Follow these Guiding Principles

Moving From	Moving To
1. Dispersed Teams	1. Collocated Teams
2. Projects	2. Releases
3. Large Projects	3. Small Initiatives
4. Part-time Allocation of Resources	4. Dedicated Team Members
5. Annual Budgeting	5. Continuous Funding
6. Project Managers	6. Team Leads
7. Functional Specialists	7. Generalizing Specialists
8. Traditional Governance	8. Agile Governance
9. Etc...	9. Etc...

In our experience this is a very powerful tool to obtain and keep organizational alignment at all levels, but in particular amongst senior management. This is a behavior management tool to ensure that management holds each other accountable for future decisions that can either help or greatly harm the efforts of the rest of the organization to be more agile. As another example, it is a well-known fact that large projects/initiatives are very risky and have high failure rates. You can improve your delivery performance and achieve ROI earlier by simply breaking the large into small. So if an executive seeks funding for a $10M initiative, we would expect their peers to point to this poster and ask, "I thought that according to Principle #3, we don't want to do large projects anymore?" It is important that management takes accountability for these principles as they relate to their daily decision making if long term positive change is to be sustained.

Implementing Improvements: Lean Change

Executing transformations using a traditional waterfall-style approach doesn't work. You cannot be successful managing your change by checklist. It would be a mistake to assume that any change that is made regarding your transformation will be permanent. Many of your process improvements won't work and will need to be changed or be rolled back. So declaring any change as "done" doesn't make sense. Instead, your change management process needs to continually reassess the effectiveness of past changes made and adjust accordingly. Figure 7.7 provides an overview of the Lean Change management cycle.

Figure 7.7. The Lean Change cycle.

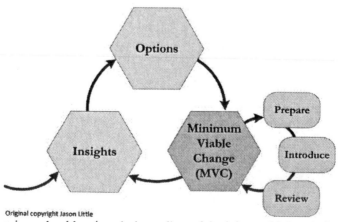

Original copyright Jason Little

Maintain a backlog/work item list of insights which are important things to understand about your organization, its people, and the type of changes desired. These insights often illustrate aspects of perceived impediments to business agility. For each insight various options are identified which might address these impediments. You then weigh each option based on how long they might take, how hard, and what the value of the option might be. What is the organization's appetite for change? You could play it safe, or be more disruptive. An example of an insight could be "Team members have difficulty focusing because they are working on multiple initiatives." An option to address this insight could be "Move team members to dedicated teams that deliver work from one common backlog."

You then treat each option to be implemented as a small "experiment", a.k.a. a minimal viable change (MVC), and follow the Lean Change management lifecycle for each:

1. **Prepare**. For each change, ensure that you have done preparatory work to plan, schedule, communicate, and to discuss the merits of chosen options with the change recipients. The people who will be living with the day-to-day outcome of the change must be actively involved with the design of the change and must pull the appropriate change(s) into their team. Pushing change into teams greatly reduces the chance that the change will stick. Change recipients should understand that change that impacts them is just an experiment. If it doesn't work (as they may be skeptical) there will be an opportunity to roll back the change or for them to try something different. For some or all of our changes we may choose to write a simple hypothesis for the expected benefit of the change. This is useful to assess if the option adopted is truly an improvement and thus should be sustained, or if the change needs to be rolled back, and potentially another option considered.

2. **Introduce**. The next step is for the affected team(s) to experiment with the change. Since we are using a lean approach to change, it is important to keep the work in progress (WIP) to a minimum. Working on too much change at the same time means that lots of things are started but nothing is getting done. Focus on a small number of changes, and keep the flow of small changes moving.

3. **Review (learn)**. At this point we monitor the effects of the change to see if it achieves the expected positive result. This review or "learn state" may be short, or may last many months. This is a key aspect of this change management approach, understanding that we don't prematurely declare "done and

success" when a change has been introduced.

4.   **Done**. If and when we consider the experiment a success and we don't need to monitor it as closely, we can move the option/experiment to a done status. At this point it is no longer an experiment and you may add further work items to your Kanban backlog to rollout the change to the rest of the enterprise, with the requisite communications, training if required, and updates to other organizational assets such as wikis or intranets.

As any change moves through these four states we visualize the status by using a Kanban board for the work in progress using four columns: Prepare, Introduce, Review, and Done. You can see an example of this at the bottom of the change canvas in Figure 7.5. As a result all changes are clearly communicated and transparent to the team. In general, post your information radiators such as Change Canvases, Moving From/To posters, Strategy Boards, and Kanban boards in public spaces to make all work visible. Embrace transparency. Of course for large distributed organizations, you will need to consider other ways to communicate effectively. Disciplined Agile provides many strategies for effective communications in complex environments.

The Lean Change approach that we have described here is a combination of structured change management techniques such as: Awareness / Desire / Knowledge / Action / Reinforcement (ADKAR), Plan/Do/Study/Adapt(Act) (PDSA) [Deming], DAD's Exploratory lifecycle and other lean delivery approaches such as Kanban. Consistent with Lean, we need to ensure that we limit work in progress (WIP). We often see agile change management teams being pressured to get everything done within a short time frame. Agile transformations are multi-year endeavors, and, as described earlier, really should be considered to be long-term continuous improvement initiatives.

Measure Your Way to Success

Part of any successful agile transformation includes design and implementation of a set of metrics applicable for the endeavor. We favor a lightweight version of a metrics approach called Goal Question Metric (GQM) to ensure that we use the appropriate metrics. Figure 7.8 shows an example of metrics design for an improvement initiative from an actual client. The idea is to consider the business goals behind your agile transformation. These should map back to the same goals in your Change Canvas as shown in Figure 7.5. For each goal, consider what questions we could ask to assess fulfillment of these goals. Then we pick a set of candidate metrics (you are unlikely to use them all) which can be used to objectively measure attainment of these goals.

When reviewing this example it should be noted that you often have multiple questions for each goal and several candidate metrics for each question. While these metrics are definitely some of our favorites, you will likely invest some time understanding which metrics make sense for you. With no metrics you are flying blind. With too many, you are flying blinded.

Designing and selecting the right metrics is a tricky endeavor. You will need to select metrics which are easy to capture, objective, and least likely to be gamed. Another approach similar to GQM is called Objectives and Key Results (OKRs) [OKR] which came from Intel, and is used by companies such as Google. It is a simplified two-factor model compared to GQM's three-factored approach. In our experience GQM's questions help focus on the business aspect of metrics before diving into a metrics solution, but, as with everything, context counts so pick the approach that makes sense for you.

Figure 7.8. Examples of metrics design using GQM.

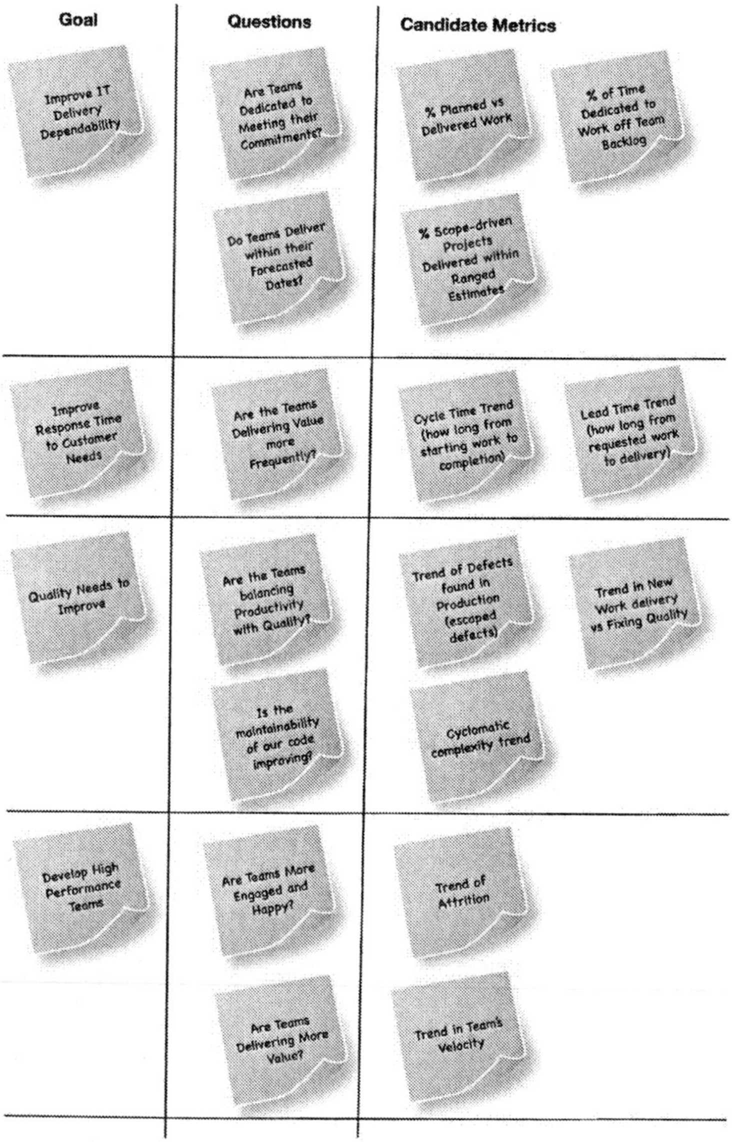

Goal	Questions	Candidate Metrics	
Improve IT Delivery Dependability	Are Teams Dedicated to Meeting their Commitment?	% Planned vs Delivered Work	% of Time Dedicated to Work off Team Backlog
	Do Teams Deliver within their Forecasted Dates?	% Scope-driven Projects Delivered within Ranged Estimates	
Improve Response Time to Customer Needs	Are the Teams Delivering Value more Frequently?	Cycle Time Trend (how long from starting work to completion)	Lead Time Trend (how long from requested work to delivery)
Quality Needs to Improve	Are the Teams balancing Productivity with Quality?	Trend of Defects found in Production (escaped defects)	Trend in New Work delivery vs Fixing Quality
	Is the maintainability of our code improving?	Cyclomatic complexity trend	
Develop High Performance Teams	Are Teams More Engaged and Happy?	Trend of Attrition	
	Are Teams Delivering More Value?	Trend in Team's Velocity	

Transformations Evolve

In the next chapter we show how your Transformation journey in practice morphs into a Continuous Improvement initiative, as transformations are never really done.

8 FROM TRANSFORMATION TO CONTINUOUS IMPROVEMENT

Attaining and sustaining business agility is a journey, not a destination. Attaining business agility is not really about transformations, although that is a common way to get started, it's really about evolving into a learning organization. In *Reinventing Organizations* Laloux says that it is very difficult to move between organizational levels without express leadership support (we believe widespread organizational support). As previously mentioned, Laloux recommends that you focus on becoming the best Amber, or best Orange, organization that you can be so as to not have to fight, and often lose to, the cultural inertia within your organization [Laloux]. In other words, focus on continuous improvement, the subject of this chapter. Your initial transformation efforts will get you going, but your continuous improvement strategy is the key to long term success.

Becoming an organization that is nimble and can continually deliver value in a rapidly changing business environment is a long-term continuous improvement endeavor. In fact, Daniel Gagnon prefers the phrase Disciplined Agile "evolution" rather than *transformation.* It would be a mistake to only fund a transformation initiative over a one-year period and set expectations that you will then be done and miraculously now declare ourselves agile. As we show in Figure 8.1, you may start with the short-term goal of this being a "transformation project" but you will find that to truly succeed you need to shift into a long-term continuous improvement (CI) strategy. As the Cynefin framework advises, in a complex adaptive system (CAS) such as your organization, behavior emerges over time. You need to probe first with experiments that are safe to fail, sense the reaction to the experiment, and then respond. The implication, as we show in Figure 8.2, is that you need to shift your efforts into continuous improvement strategy.

Agile and lean have always had built-in practices for continuous improvement at the team level. However, what is less understood is the need for improvement at the enterprise level. We find that Lean is well understood by business and indeed we often see agile transformation initiatives driven from pressure from the business stakeholders to become more lean or agile in order to dovetail with their business process improvements. The implications are that your agile transformation initiatives should really be about continuous improvement which is aligned with your business process initiatives and that the real goal is long-term growth and adaptation.

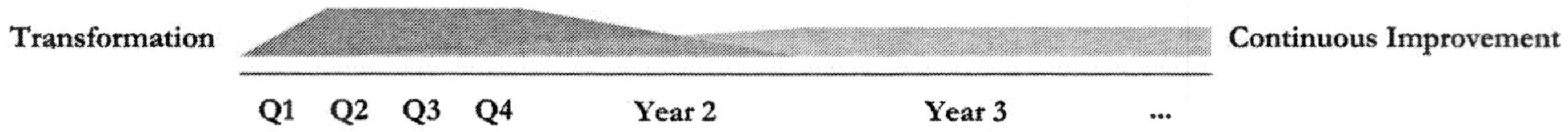

Figure 8.1. The evolution from transformation to continuous

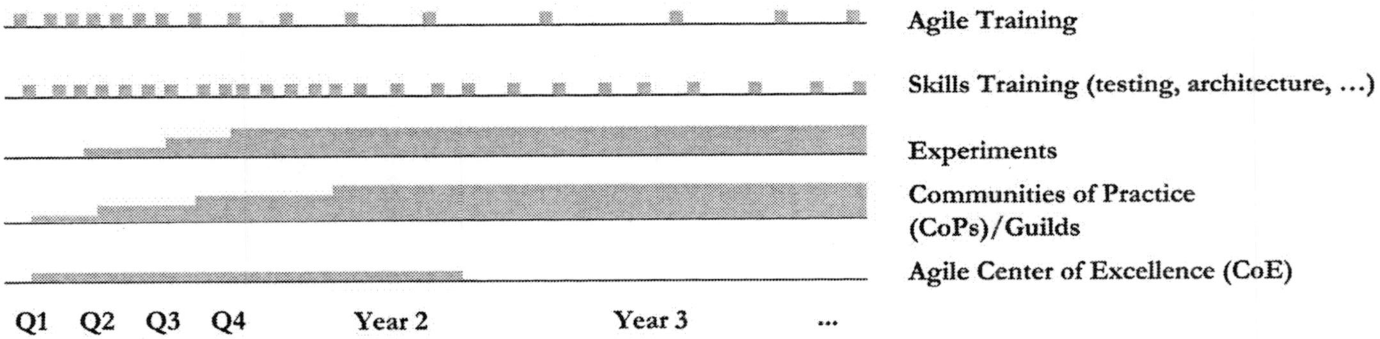

Figure 8.2. Continuous improvement activities over time.

167

Why Continuous Improvement?

There are several reasons why you want to have a continuous improvement program within your organization:

1. **Shorten the time from idea to implementation**. Improvement ideas can come from anyone, at any time, from anywhere in your organization. As a result you want to have organizational mechanisms to identify and explore those ideas so that they get to the person(s) most suitable to implement them quickly.

2. **Increase skills and knowledge sharing**. The high-collaboration environments that are typical of agile teams are wonderful for sharing skills and knowledge within each team, but fellow team members aren't the only people within your organization that you can learn from. An important goal of a continuous improvement program is to motivate and enable people to share their skills and knowledge outside of their immediate team. You can do this through strategies such as communities of practice, online discussion forums, practitioner presentations and many others.

3. **Maximize your "failure ROI"**. A fundamental of lean thinking is to learn from your failures, to treat each "failure" as an opportunity to improve. Having said that, every team doesn't need to experience all of the same failures. One team, or a handful of teams in some cases, can fail in similar ways and then share those learnings with others. This way other teams can avoid that type of failure and thereby increase the value of the learnings to your organization. But we can only do that when it's safe to fail and better yet recognize that failures should be celebrated and the learnings shared with others.

4. **Increase the opportunity for radical improvements**. The challenge with the Japanese concept of kaizen, which is to continuously make small incremental improvements, is that you can get on an improvement path that will never lead to a quantum leap in your process. Yes, things are getting better, but you may be missing opportunities to make things a lot better. For example a team following the Scrum-based Agile/Basic lifecycle may never identify the strategy of continuous deployment (CD) on their own because having a two-week iteration may preclude the idea of releasing several times a day into production. Yet, if people on your team were to hear about other teams in your organization working that way, they might soon choose to start experimenting with CD techniques. This in turn could lead to the idea of abandoning time-boxed iterations and moving to something much closer to DA's Continuous Delivery lifecycle.

In short, your organization needs a strategy for communicating potential improvements across teams. Ideally the flow of work should be streamlined to make it as easy as possible for teams to learn from one another. Your true goal is to have an organization that works as a community that shares ideas and improves together.

Optimize (the Whole) Flow

Unfortunately most agile conferences that we attend address continuous improvement practices focused on optimization at the individual and team levels. The most popular continuous improvement strategy at these levels is a scheduled team retrospective wherein the team meets to discuss what they are doing well, not so well, and what actions they can take to improve their performance. As we show in Figure 8.3 to be truly effective we need to expand the scope of our continuous improvement efforts to address the enterprise level (with the aim to become a DAE). We need to think about how we share learnings across teams, vertically from individual to the enterprise, as well as horizontally between business, IT, and other organizational areas such as marketing and finance.

Figure 8.3. The scope of continuous improvement.

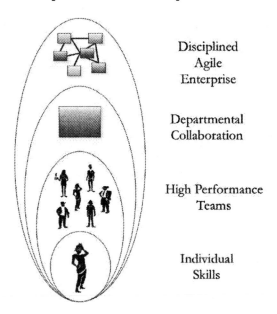

Disciplined
Agile
Enterprise

Departmental
Collaboration

High Performance
Teams

Individual
Skills

The Process

The Continuous Improvement goal diagram shown in Figure 8.4 overviews the potential activities associated with disciplined agile continuous improvement. These activities may have been traditionally performed by, or at least supported by, a process improvement team (sometimes referred to as a Software Engineering Process Group, or SEPG). Some of these practices can be performed by Centers of Excellence (CoEs) and supported by your Communities of Practice (CoPs) (if any).

The process factors that you need to consider for continuous improvement are:

1. **Identify improvements**. There are several ways that your process improvement group can support the identification of potential improvements within your organization. One of the more effective strategies is to help teams adopt the practice of holding regular retrospectives where the team purposefully collaborates to identify potential areas of improvement. However, this only works when the people involved are a real team who work together regularly and they want to change. Although it is common for DAD teams to hold retrospectives this is often a new concept for enterprise architecture teams, IT governance teams, data management teams, and so on. We also get very good traction with value stream mapping and brainstorming sessions, which invariably proves to be far more effective than the traditional approach of creating current and proposed (business) process models that rarely seem to result in lasting acceptance of the proposed new way of working.

2. **Share improvements**. As you can see there are multiple ways that you can share improvement ideas between teams, many of them being free or at least very inexpensive to implement. We've had very good experiences with internal discussion forums such as Jive or ActiveBoard, practitioner presentations (often called lunch and learns) where someone presents their learnings to others, lean coffee sessions where people voluntarily meet at a regular time to share ideas, and communities of practice (sometimes called guilds) who purposely collaborate to educate themselves on a given topic.

Figure 8.4. The Continuous Improvement process blade goal diagram.

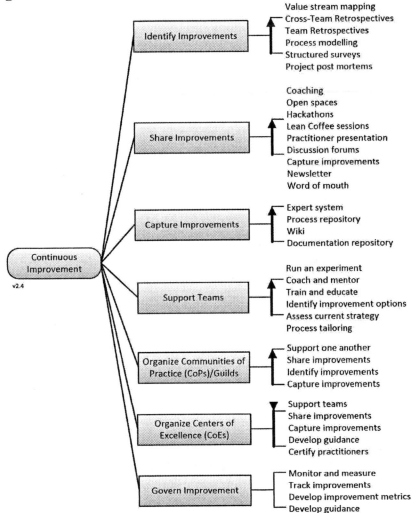

3. **Capture improvements.** There are various ways that identified improvements may be captured to retain them over time. Possible strategies include describing each learning in a document and then managing that document in a documentation repository such as Sharepoint or more simply in a shared folder; capturing the learnings in a shared wiki such as Confluence; describing your evolving process using a process repository such as Stages or Rational Method Composer; or via an expert system

such as Enterprise Transformation Advisor.

4. **Support teams**. Your process improvement team can help others to adopt process improvement techniques through training, education, and coaching. They can also facilitate team assessments and retrospectives (a great idea is to co-facilitate a few retrospectives with someone on the team to transfer those skills to them). A very effective strategy is to help a team run a process improvement experiment or two, particularly in situations where the team isn't being supported by a coach. This helps them see that they can safely try new ideas within their environment for a few iterations to determine whether it works for them or not. Many teams, particularly those new to agile, often do not feel empowered to run such experiments and thus need help to do so.

5. **Organize Communities of Practice (CoPs)/Guilds**. A Community of Practice (CoP) is a collection of people who share a craft or profession who have banded together to 'learn' from each other to develop themselves and their organization. We've seen CoPs for testing, architecture, agile/lean, business analysis, technical debt, and many others. CoPs will often perform the activities called out by the Identify Improvements, Share Improvements, Capture Improvements, and Support Teams process factors. A CoP will often start up when one or more practitioners within your organization recognize the need for it, although sometimes it may also start to support the efforts of a corresponding Center of Excellence (CoE). Participation in a CoP is typically voluntary.

6. **Organize Centers of Excellence (CoEs)**. A Center of Excellence (CoE) is a group of people with specialized skills and expertise whose job is to provide leadership and purposely disseminate that knowledge within your org anization. CoEs are often created by an organization

> ### A Disciplined Agile CoE
> Diana Popescu heads up the DA CoE for ICBC in Vancouver. Her title is Manager, Disciplined Agile and Continuous Improvement. Mark has been their external Enterprise Coach, working with a mix of internal and external Team Coaches. At time of writing the DA CoE was rolling out Guilds (CoPs) for Agile Testing and Team Leads, with Agile Architecture coming next.

to support the adoption of a new technology or technique, and in fact the creation of an Agile CoE is often a key component of your organization's overall Agile transformation efforts. Over the years we've seen CoEs for object technology (particularly in the 90s when it was new to most companies), solution architecture, testing automation, and of course agile/lean. Participation as a member of a CoE will be part of, or the entire job for someone.

7. **Govern improvement.** It is very common for senior management to want to know whether or not the organization is benefiting from your investment in adopting agile and lean techniques (or other potential improvements for that matter), how much things are improving, and how widespread the adoption is. The implication is that there needs to be some way to monitor and report on, preferably in a lightweight and streamlined manner, the improvement activities.

Becoming Self-Sufficient

Using skilled and experienced external Enterprise and Team Coaches will definitely accelerate your agile transformation and reduce overall risk for this critical organizational change endeavor. However, you will want to have a strategy in place to transfer your dependence on external guidance to internal. Your knowledge transfer should focus on these areas:

1. **Moving from external to internal coaching.** Very early in your transformation you should designate internal enterprise and team coaches for knowledge transfer from your external coaches. These people will be part of your Disciplined Agile CoE.

2. **Moving from Centers of Excellence (CoEs) to Communities of Practice (CoPs).** Initially your CoE will be tasked with guiding your development in the areas of agile training, skills training, conducting improvement experiments and establishing CoPs. Figure 8.4 shows how the work is done incrementally over time to incrementally conduct basic agile as well as specialized skills training. Simultaneously the CoE will facilitate change experiments to incrementally roll out structural and behavioral organizational change. You will also establish CoPs incrementally.

3. **Discontinuing your CoE.** Over time you will want to transition the responsibility for learning and continuous improvement to the CoPs. As shown in Figure 8.4 as you establish sustainable and institutionalized agile and lean cultural change you may find that you no longer need a dedicated Disciplined Agile CoE. You may decide to keep your CoE in place over time, especially in larger organizations with the focus over time shifting from agile transformation to continuous improvement. This is often the case for organizations that continuously look for opportunities

for business optimization with lean techniques such as those promoted by Lean Six Sigma.

Patterns for Successful Transformations/Improvement Initiatives

At Scott Ambler + Associates we have been fortunate enough to have helped steer many Agile and Lean transformation efforts around the world. Additionally we have invested much time in learning from the experiences of others. We have observed some reoccurring patterns that can either lead to success or failure. Often failure leads to regression back to previous habits. Some have described this as the "rubber band effect" whereby the organizational memory of an organization tends to pull it back to its historical behavior.

Patterns for Success

Have a roadmap. As we have described earlier, it is important to have an overall roadmap for your transformation initiative that is communicated and well understood at all levels of the organization. This includes not only through IT but also the business.

> **Don't ignore the "pressurized middle"**
> In our transformation experience we have learned not to ignore middle management and make sure that they understand what their new role will be in an agile organization. In the act of top-down transformation and bottom up incremental enablement of agile and lean teams it is easy to forget that middle management likely is experiencing some anxiety about their own future. As a result they are likely to either ignore what is going on around them, or worse, look for ways to undermine the success of your transformation. The sooner they understand their new role and the fear and uncertainty is removed, the sooner they can become enablers of change rather than resisters. Our approach is to give them basic Disciplined Agile training, as well as a one-day workshop called "Disciplined Agile for Managers" which clearly educates them on how they can help.

Genuine and visible leadership support. We expect leadership to exhibit the following:

- **Patience.** We have been asked in the past to commit to completing a transformation in three months. Not possible. True transformations take years, and even then they evolve into a continuous improvement journey. Process improvement never ends.

- **Willingness to invest.** Transformations require investment for things like training, coaching, workplace design, relocation, and possibly restructuring depending on management's tolerance and budget for change.
- **Engagement.** Leadership needs to participate and engage at every opportunity. Some of your people will see adoption as a fad and will wait for it to pass. You need to reinforce the message that the change is fundamental and structural. People who do not believe in the sustainability of the change can sometimes work to undermine the change so that it goes away quicker and whereupon they can return to the way they "always did things".
- **Actively rewarding and recognizing success.** With a decent coach you will likely be able to demonstrate success on your early agile teams very quickly. Make sure that you celebrate the success and provide recognition visible to everyone. You should also have a preference towards team over individual awards as individual awards can encourage competition within the team and discourage good team dynamics.
- **Creation of a safe and nurturing environment.** Work to encourage innovation, experimentation, and acceptance of failure as learning opportunities. Teams will be reluctant to embrace self-organization and try new things on their own initiative if they fear reprisal for mistakes made in good faith.
- **Communicate, communicate, communicate.** Fear and uncertainty related to change can quickly sink your transformation. Use techniques such as town hall meetings, newsletters, lean coffees, wikis, and post information radiators where everyone can see them.

Patterns that Typically Lead to Failure

We have run into several common anti-patterns that tend to cause agile improvement efforts to fail:

1. **Disguising a cost cutting initiative as an "agile transformation".** We have unfortunately seen transformations used as an excuse to let large numbers of people go in the name of agile. We have heard statements made like "agile doesn't need project managers, business analysts, or middle managers" without knowledge or understanding of how to fill the void left behind when they go. In these situations we have seen that while they don't

hesitate to cut costs for salaries, they don't invest in training and coaching to help the people on the new agile teams to understand how to be effective in the new world.

2. **Buying into one process and believing it is equally applicable to all situations.** Scrum is not ideal for all situations, neither is Extreme Programming (XP), Lean, nor SAFe. They are all extremely appropriate in certain situations. Using a flexible framework, such as the Disciplined Agile framework, that can be suited to all types of initiatives and technologies simplifies the task of tailoring the approach to your context.

3. **Believing that you can buy Agile or DevOps from a vendor.** What you very likely need is a process framework appropriate for you with a selection of lightweight tooling, not a prescriptive process and heavyweight tooling from a vendor.

4. **Unqualified coaches.** As we described earlier, it is very important to invest in coaches that have done this many times before whether you are looking for an Enterprise or Team coach. You cannot afford to fail and you don't want coaches failing and learning on your dime.

5. **Treating this like a project, not a journey.** Transformations really should be considered continuous improvement initiatives, not projects that have a fixed end date. You will never truly be "done". You need to continuously sharpen the blade [Covey].

6. **Pushing change onto people.** Yes, sometimes you need to force the issue, particularly when your face an existential crisis, and force/push change on people. However, change is significantly more sticky when people accept the need to change, are actively involved with identifying the change, and then willingly pull potential changes into their team to experiment with them and see how to make them work in practice.

9 IN CONCLUSION

We have covered a lot of ground in this book. Our goal was not to write an executive agile "playbook" as there is no set of plays that will be suitable for your unique context. Rather, we have tried to show the complexities of a truly agile enterprise and describe the principles that can help turn your organizational tractor into a race car for a Formula One track into which the world is quickly evolving.

First the Bad News

The Phoenix Project, Joy Inc., and other truly great reads paint pictures and tell stories that teach powerful lessons and convey certain agile mindsets required for DevOps and creating joyful organizations and teams. These are great books, and very approachable. However, what worked for them might not work for you. The really hard work begins when you try to apply those lessons for your specific and far ranging challenges. If your environment doesn't match those described in these books you are left to figure it out yourself. Additionally, each book is usually focused on one or two key messages, albeit in great detail. The daunting challenge of this book has been to point out all the moving parts of agile enterprises and how to nurture these complex adaptive systems for optimal efficiency. Yes, the unfortunate reality is that this is hard. Perhaps if nothing else, we have helped move you from not knowing what you don't know, to knowing what you don't know. This is progress! Some of your challenges will include:

- **Complexity.** Solution delivery is complex. DevOps is complex. IT is complex. Your overall organization is complex. What makes it even more challenging is that your people, teams, organization, and the world around them is constantly learning and adapting.
- **No silver bullet.** There are no quick fixes, no silver bullets, no one process or scaling framework to rule all regardless of the marketing rhetoric surrounding them. Every person, every team, and every organization is unique.
- **It will take time.** This is a multi-year journey. And when you have achieved what you perceive to be true business agility you will need to evolve to a long-term continuous improvement approach as everything around you will continue to change.
- **It requires sustained investment.** Achieving your

transformation goals will take a material investment. In all likelihood you will want to seek help from external partners that have a record of long-term success with agile transformations. While the required investment will decrease over time, you will need to continue your visible support for continuous improvement in the interest of "sharpening the blade".

- **It requires courage and commitment**. Every single success story, every single one, starts with the organizational decision to do the hard work to get better. And every single one eventually recognizes that improvement is a way of life, not a project.

- **There will be casualties**. Some people won't like this change and will need to move on to other opportunities (and yes, for some people this won't be voluntary). People will need to want to change, you can't force it upon them. Fortunately there are proven strategies to increase the odds that they will want to jump onboard.

- **Change must be pulled not pushed**. You need to pull agility and discipline into your organization, you can't push change onto people and hope it will stick.

- **Beware snake oil sales people**. The agile community has been seeded with "Certified Masters" that have received two entire days of training, or "Professional Coaches" that have received four, and sometimes five, days of training in their flavor of agile. Many of these people incidentally have no background in IT! There are also some great people out there who are experienced and who can help, but their designations, if they have any, are generally not good indications of that. In all likelihood if you have had the perseverance to read this entire book, you have more knowledge than many of the coaches that offer to help you. Verify experience, check references, and expect better than the run of the mill.

Now the Good News

Sustainable transformational change is hard, yet achievable. As you have read from our stories of successful agile transformations around the world, organizations are indeed effecting necessary transformational change. Key success criteria include: using a structured experiment-based change management technique such as Lean Change, using the Disciplined Agile framework to guide your optimizations, and using experienced coaches that understand both.

Yes this can be hard, but DA reduces the complexity that you face by making the process issues that you face explicit, and more importantly provides choices and trade-offs so that you can develop, and then evolve, an approach that makes sense for you. DA is the only framework available that collects and organizes your potential strategies in one place so that you can easily see what options are available and make the best choices for your context. Better choices lead to better outcomes.

Understanding what is in the framework, where to find things, and what choices are best for certain situations requires an investment in learning. As we have described, certifying your people and expecting your external partners to do the same validates that your teams, enterprise groups, and business stakeholders do indeed understand, and have actually successfully applied the appropriate strategies for optimizing your enterprise.

Some advice regarding certification:

- Expect much from your consultants, such as proven experience and understanding of the strategies in this book
- There are a lot of great practitioners and coaches out there who could easily come up to speed on DA. You may need to invest in your people so as to get them on a more effective track
- DA certification is enterprise-worthy certification without the enterprise cost associated with some other certifications

What Next?

If you agree with the principles we described in Chapter 2 such as pragmatism, enterprise awareness, choice is good, and context counts then hopefully you can understand that for many if not most organizations Disciplined Agile just makes sense. You may wish to learn more if you find yourself in any of these situations:

- You are just beginning an agile enterprise transformation
- You have been doing Scrum, Kanban, XP or some other mainstream methods at the team level but haven't yet engaged overall IT and the enterprise
- You have been "doing agile" for several years but aren't getting the expected benefits you were promised
- You have tried SAFe but have begun to realize that just layering a prescriptive scaling framework on top of a traditional organization won't win the race to business agility

How do you get started? As we described in Chapter 7, we typically recommend engaging an experienced, certified DA Partner to first conduct a short 3-4 day assessment to determine where you actually are, what's working for you, and what isn't. The result should be an implementation plan and roadmap for beginning your DA transformation journey.

If you are not ready to move forward with Disciplined Agile an alternative would be to take a deeper dive into the topics in this book by investing in a Disciplined Agile Executive workshop. The format is to spend the morning baselining a fundamental understanding of what Disciplined Agile is, the current state of business agility, and what other organizations are doing to remain competitive. The content is customized based on your organization's understanding of these topics. Then in the afternoon we take a deeper dive into topics that are of particular interest to your organization. The outcome is a set of actionable ideas that you can pursue to accelerate your journey to business agility.

You're Not Alone

There is a rich and growing Disciplined Agile community to get involved with. Here are some resources you should get to know:
1. **DisciplinedAgileConsortium.org**. The Disciplined Agile Consortium (DAC) is responsible for evolving DA, providing courseware, and is the certification body for DA. DAC provides frequent webinars on all aspects of DA complimentary to its members.
2. **Certified Disciplined Agile Partners**. If you want some help moving your organization toward business agility we recommend engaging a certified DA partner. They are listed in the Partner section of the DAC website.
3. **DisciplinedAgileDelivery.com**. The DA website provides a rich resource of DA content as well as a frequent blog of topics regarding DA.
4. **LinkedIn Discussion forum**. This discussion forum is the place for all kinds of topics related to DA.
5. **ScottAmbler.com**. While we certainly recommend working with a local certified DA partner, Scott Ambler + Associates would of course be pleased to help you. We have a long history of steering successful DA transformations for organizations around the world. We would be pleased to share references and case studies. We have also become quite effective with conducting large scale transformations using a

blend of on-site and remote work. We also do a lot of "train the trainer" and "coach the coach" engagements to enable larger organizations to scale their improvement strategy.

To Wrap Up

We are passionate about what we do. The primary reason is, every time, every single time we work with an organization, we see visible positive change across the board. When we initially go into new clients we typically do an assessment whereupon we quickly discover where problems lie. It could be any number of things including poor morale and attrition, low productivity, poor quality, excessive waste, competitive pressures, or dissatisfied stakeholders. However, what we have seen over and over again with successful Disciplined Agile transformations is happier teams, happier middle management, happier enterprise support teams, happier executives, and most importantly, delighted business stakeholders.

This book has provided the guidance you need to create a vision for change, with supplemental lean change management guidance for steering your transformation effort to effect this change. Now that you have a solid understanding of how the parts can fit together in order to achieve true business agility, this book can become a reference as you incrementally start to make the changes required to optimize your enterprise. Good luck on your journey, and let us know if we can help.

Mark & Scott, July 2017

We Need Your Help

If you liked this book, we hope that you will post a positive review on Amazon for it. Many people rely on reviews to decide whether to purchase a book, so this would be a huge help for us. Thank you in advance for taking time out of your busy schedule to help us!

However, if you don't like the book, we'd love to have a chance to discuss any issues that you have. Please reach out to us at feedback@disciplinedagileconsortium

REFERENCES AND RESOURCES

[AgileContracts] *Agile Contracts Home Page*. AgileContracts.org

[AgileData] *Agile Data Home Page*. AgileData.org

[AgileDocumentation] *Agile/Lean Documentation: Strategies for Agile Software Development*. AgileModeling.com/essays/agileDocumentation.htm

[Amazon] *Inside the Mind of Jeff Bezos*. Fast Company, August 2004, FastCompany.com/50541/inside-mind-jeff-bezos-4

[AmblerLines2012] Disciplined *Agile Delivery: A Practitioner's Guide to Agile Software Delivery in the Enterprise*. Scott Ambler and Mark Lines, 2012, IBM Press.

[Anderson] *Kanban: Successful Evolutionary Change for Your Technology Business*. David J. Anderson, 2010, Blue Hole Press.

[AoS2016]. *2016 Agility at Scale Survey Results*. Ambysoft.com/surveys/agileAtScale2016.html

[Appelo2010] *Management 3.0: Leading Agile Developers, Developing Agile Leaders*. Jurgen Appelo, 2010, Addison-Wesley Professional.

[Appelo2016] *Managing for Happiness: Games, Tools, and Practices to Motivate Any Team*. Jurgen Appelo, 2016, Wiley.

[APIFirst] *API-First Home Page*. Api-first.com

[Argyris] *Double Loop Learning in Organizations*. Chris Argyris, Harvard Business Review, September 1977, hbr.org/1977/09/double-loop-learning-in-organizations

[Beck] *Extreme Programming Explained: Embrace Change (2nd Edition)*. Kent Beck and Cynthia Andres, 2004, Addison Wesley Publishing.

[Borthwick] *Tech is Eating Media. Now What?* medium.com/@Borthwick/time-for-a-change-2be08d01d40

[BritishAirways] *British Airways IT Outage: What Went Wrong with its datacentre?* computerweekly.com/news/450420405/The-British-Airways-IT-outage-What-went-wrong-with-its-datacentre

[BRUF] *Examining the "Big Requirements Up Front (BRUF) Approach"*. AgileModeling.com/essays/examiningBRUF.htm

[Bungay] *The Art of Action: How Leaders Close the Gaps Between Plans, Actions, and Results*. Stephen Bungay, 2010, Nicholas Brealey Publishing.

[CAS] *Complex Adaptive Systems*. en.wikipedia.org/wiki/Complex_adaptive_system

[ChaosReport] *Standish Group Chaos Report*. StandishGroup.com/outline

[CMMI] *The Disciplined Agile Framework: A Pragmatic Approach to Agile Maturity*. DisciplinedAgileConsortium.org/resources/Whitepapers/DA-CMMI-Crosstalk-201607.pdf

[COBIT] *COBIT 5 Home Page.* isaca.org/COBIT/pages/default.aspx

[Cockburn] *Heart of Agile Home Page.* http://heartofagile.com/

[Covey] *The 7 Habits of Highly Effective People: Powerful Lessons in Personal Change 25th Anniversary Edition.* Stephen R. Covey 2013, Simon & Schuster

[CreativityInc] *Creativity, Inc. Overcoming the Unseen Forces That Stand in the Way of True Inspiration.* Ed Catmull and Amy Wallace, 2014, Random House Canada.

[Cynefin] *A Leader's Framework for Decision Making.* David J. Snowden and Mary E. Boone, Harvard Business Review, November 2007, hbr.org/2007/11/a-leaders-framework-for-decision-making

[DABlog] *Disciplined Agile Delivery Home Page.* DisciplinedAgileDelivery.com

[DAC] *Disciplined Agile Consortium Home Page.* DisciplinedAgileConsortium.org

[DADRoles] *Roles on DAD Teams.* http://DisciplinedAgileDelivery.com/roles-on-dad-teams/

[DAMA] *DAMA Guide to the Data Management Body of Knowledge.* Technicspub.com/dmbok/

[DAManifesto] Disciplined Agile Manifesto. DisciplinedAgileDelivery.com/disciplinedagilemanifesto/

[DavenportHarris] *Competing on Analytics: The New Science of Winning.* Thomas H. Davenport and Jeanne G. Harris, 2007, Harvard Business School Press.

[DBRefactoring] *Refactoring Databases: Evolutionary Database Design.* Scott W. Ambler and Pramod J. Sadalage, 2006, Addison Wesley.

[Deloitte] *Deloitte Insight: Over 100,000 Legal Roles to be Automated.* https://www.legaltechnology.com/latest-news/deloitte-insight-100000-legal-roles-to-be-automated/

[DeepRoot] *Personal details of nearly 200 million US citizens exposed.* http://www.bbc.com/news/technology-40331215

[DeMarco] *Slack: Getting Past Burnout, Busywork, and the Myth of Total Efficiency.* Tom DeMarco, 2002, Crown Business.

[Deming] *The New Economics for Industry, Government, Education.* W. Edwards Deming, 2002, MIT Press.

[DevSecOps] *The DevSecOps Manifesto.* DevSecOps.org

[GenSpec] Generalizing Specialists: Improving Your IT Career Skills. AgileModeling.com/essays/generalizingSpecialists.htm

[Gilb] *Competitive Engineering: A Handbook For Systems Engineering, Requirements Engineering, and Software Engineering Using Planguage.* Tom Gilb, 2005, Butterworth-Heinemann.

[Goals] *Process Goals.* DisciplinedAgileDelivery.com/process-goals/

[Google] *Five Keys to a Successful Google Team.* Julia Rozovsky. https://rework.withgoogle.com/blog/five-keys-to-a-successful-google-team/

[Heartland] *Heartland: Largest Data Breach Ever.* csoonline.com/article/2123599/malware-cybercrime/heartland---largest-data-breach-ever-.html

[HopeFraser] *Beyond Budgeting: How Managers Can Break Free From the Annual Performance Trap.* Jeremy Hope and Robin Fraser, 2003, Harvard Business Press.

[IBM] *IBM CEO Ginni flouts £75 travel crackdown, rides Big Blue chopper.* theregister.co.uk/2017/05/19/ibm_ceo_flouts_travel_restriction_in_chopper/

[Kim]. *DevOps Cookbook.* RealGeneKim.me/devops-cookbook/

[Kerievsky] *Modern Agile.* ModernAgile.org/

[Kruchten] *The Rational Unified Process: An Introduction 3rd Edition.* Philippe Kruchten, 2003, Addison Wesley Professional.

[Laloux] *Reinventing Organizations: A Guide to Creating Organizations Inspired by the Next Stage in Human Consciousness.* Frederic Laloux, 2014, Nelson Parker Publishing.

[LargeTeams] *Large Agile Teams.* DisciplinedAgileDelivery.com/agility-at-scale/large-agile-teams/

[LeanAnalytics] *Lean Analytics: Use Data to Build a Better Startup Faster.* Alistair Croll and Benjamin Yoskovitz, 2003, O'Reilly Media, Inc.

[LeanChange1] *The Lean Change Method: Managing Agile Organizational Transformation Using Kanban, Kotter, and Lean Startup Thinking.* Jeff Anderson, 2013, Createspace.

[LeanChange2] *Lean Change Management Home Page.* LeanChange.org

[LeanEnterprise] *Lean Enterprise: How High Performance Organizations Innovate at Scale.* Jez Humble, Joanne Molesky, and Barry O'Reilly, 2015, O'Reilly Media, Inc.

[Lego] *The Incredible Manufacturing Process That Brings Us Lego.* rcrwireless.com/20160921/big-data-analytics/lego-automated-factory-tag31-tag99

[Leybourn] *Domains of Agility.* TheAgileDirector.com/article/2016/11/24/domains-of-agility/

[Lifecycles] *Full Agile Delivery Lifecycles.* DisciplinedAgileDelivery.com/lifecycle/

[LinesAmbler2015] *Disciplined Agile Delivery: A Practitioner's Guide to Agile Software Delivery in the Enterprise.* Scott W. Ambler and Mark Lines, 2012, IBM Press.

[MarketingManifesto] *Agile Marketing Manifesto Home Page.* AgileMarketingManifesto.org/

[MartinOsterling] *Value Stream Mapping: How to Visualize Work and Align Leadership for Organizational Transformation.* Karen Martin, and Mike Osterling, 2015, McGraw Hill

[Manifesto] *The Agile Manifesto.* AgileManifesto.org

[McKinsey] *The Alchemy of Growth: Practical Insights for Building the Enduring Enterprise.* Mehrdad Baghai, Steve Coley, and David White, 2000, Basic Books.

[McKinseyMarketing] *Agile Marketing: A Step-by-Step Guide.* McKinsey.com/business-functions/marketing-and-sales/our-insights/agile-marketing-a-step-by-step-guide

[Mismatch] *The Cultural Impedance Mismatch Between Data Professionals and Developers.* Agiledata.org/essays/culturalImpedanceMismatch.html

[Netflix] *Lessons Netflix Learned from the AWS Outage.* medium.com/netflix-techblog/lessons-netflix-learned-from-the-aws-outage-deefe5fd0c04

[OKR] OKR en.wikipedia.org/wiki/OKR

[PDCA] PDCA en.wikipedia.org/wiki/PDCA

[Pink] *Drive: The Surprising Truth About What Motivates Us.* Daniel H. Pink, 2011, Riverhead Books.

[PMI] *PMBoK Guide and Standards.* pmi.org/pmbok-guide-standards

[Poppendieck] *The Lean Mindset: Ask the Right Questions.* Mary and Tom Poppendieck, 2013, Addison Wesley Professional.

[Prince] *Prince2.* Axelos.com/best-practice-solutions/prince2

[Reinertsen] *The Principles of Product Development Flow: Second Generation Lean Product Development.* Donald G. Reinertsen, 2012, Celeritis Publishing.

[Ries] *The Lean Startup: How Today's Entrepreneurs Use Continuous Innovation to Create Radically Successful Businesses.* Eric Ries, 2011, Crown Business.

[Rugged] *The Rugged Manifesto.* RuggedSoftware.org

[SchwaberBeedle] *Agile Software Development with SCRUM.* Ken Schwaber and Mike Beedle, 2001, Pearson.

[ScrumGuide] *The Scrum Guide.* Schwaber and Sutherland, July 2016.

[SenseRespond] *Sense & Respond: How Successful Organizations Listen to Customers and Create New Products Continuously.* Jeff Gothelf and Josh Seiden, 2017, Harvard Business Review Press

[Sheridan] *Joy, Inc.: How We Built a Workplace People Love.* Richard Sheridan, 2014, Portfolio Publishing.

[Target] *Target Customers' Card Data Said to be at Risk After Store Thefts.* csoonline.com/article/2134248/data-protection/target-customers--39--card-data-said-to-be-at-risk-after-store-thefts.html

[TechDebt] *11 Strategies for Dealing with Technical Debt.* DisciplinedAgileDelivery.com/technical-debt/

[Tuckman] *Tuckman's Stages of Group Development.* en.wikipedia.org/wiki/Tuckman%27s_stages_of_group_development

ACRONYMS AND ABBREVIATIONS

AD	Agile Data
ADKAR	Awareness Desire Knowledge Action Reinforcement
AI	Artificial Intelligence
AM	Agile Modeling
AO	Architecture Owner
BDD	Behavior Driven Development
BI	Business Intelligence
BMUF	Big Modeling Up Front
BoK	Body of Knowledge or Book of Knowledge
CapEx	Capital Expense
CAS	Complex Adaptive System
CI	Continuous Integration –or– Continuous Improvement
CD	Continuous Deployment
CM	Configuration Management
CMMI	Capability Maturity Model Integration
COBIT	Control Objectives for Information and Related Technologies
CoE	Center of Expertise/Excellence
CoP	Community of Practice
DA	Disciplined Agile
DAE	Disciplined Agile Enterprise
DAIT	Disciplined Agile Information Technology
DAMA	Data Management Association
DevOps	Development-Operations
DW	Data Warehouse
EA	Enterprise Architect or Enterprise Architecture
FASB	Financial Accounting Standards Board
FTE	Full Time Employee
GQM	Goal Question Metric
HR	Human Resources
JBGE	Just Barely Good Enough
KM	Knowledge Management
KPI	Key Performance Indicator
IASA	International Association of Software Architects
IASB	International Accounting Standards Board
ISO	International Organization for Standardization
IT	Information Technology
ITIL	Information Technology Infrastructure Library
LoB	Line of Business
MMR	Minimum Marketable Release
MTBD	Mean Time Between Deployments

MVC	Minimum Viable Change
MVP	Minimum Viable Product
OKR	Objectives and Key Results
OpEx	Operating Expense
Ops	Operations
PCIDSS	Payment Card Industry Data Security Standard
PDSA	Plan Do Study Act
PMI	Project Management Institute
PMO	Project Management Office
PO	Product Owner
PMI	Project Management Institute
ROI	Return On Investment
SAFe	Scaled Agile Framework
SEMAT	Software Engineering Method and Theory
SEPG	Software Engineering Process Group
SoD	Separation of Duties
TFS	Team Foundation Server
TDD	Test Driven Development
UX	User Experience
VSM	Value Stream Mapping
WIP	Work in Progress
XP	Extreme Programming

INDEX

ABOUT THE AUTHORS

Scott W. Ambler is the Senior Consulting Partner of Scott Ambler + Associates, working with organizations around the world to help them improve their software processes. He provides training, coaching, and mentoring in disciplined agile and lean strategies at both the project and organization level.  Scott is the founder of the *Agile Modeling (AM), Agile Data (AD), Disciplined Agile Delivery (DAD)*, and *Enterprise Unified Process (EUP) methodologies.* He is the (co-)author of several books, including *Disciplined Agile Delivery, Refactoring Databases, Agile Modeling, Agile Database Techniques, The Object Primer 3rd Edition*, and *The Enterprise Unified Process.* Scott blogs about DAD at DisciplinedAgileDelivery.com. Scott is also a *Founding Member of the Disciplined Agile Consortium (DAC)*, the certification body for disciplined agile.

Mark Lines is Managing Partner at Scott Ambler + Associates. He is an Enterprise Agile Coach and co-creator of the Disciplined Agile Delivery framework. Mark is co-author with Scott Ambler of *Disciplined Agile Delivery: A Practitioner's Guide to Agile Software Delivery in the Enterprise* and an *Introduction to Disciplined Agile Delivery.* Mark helps clients around the world  transform from traditional to lean and agile enterprises. He is a frequent speaker at industry conferences and blogs about DAD at DisciplinedAgileDelivery.com. He is also a founding member and President of the *Disciplined Agile Consortium (DAC)*, the certification body for Disciplined Agile.